"Former British soldier Bernard O'... ...rved in Northern Ireland durin... ...Now, he has written a book ... ...typical squaddie – a reality ... ...d the rule of law were oft... ...which O'Mahoney writes be... ...to the heroic body of men depicted in th... ...ings of Andy McNab and other Boys' Own-style adventures. Instead, the antics of the author and his brother-in-arms are described unblinkingly, habitual violence and the harassment of the civilian population apparently central to military life . . . *Soldier of the Queen* is recommended reading." *Hot Press*

"The camp was full of posters of Bobby Sands with slogans like "Slimmer of the Year" cut from newspapers and pasted onto them. Bernard admits however that this bravado covered an undercurrent of fear of relatiations." *Sunday Independent*

"This is the sometimes-shocking true story of one man's determination to get home again alive and how civilised values come to be the victim in this struggle. While it will be found by some to be distasteful the strength of this account lies in its honesty and in how the author never tries to hide the truth of what he was, nor offer easy excuses. Its uniqueness also lies in the fact that most previous accounts of army life in Northern Ireland were written by members of elite or specialist units. This is the viewpoint of the ordinary "squaddie". *Garda Review*

Bernard O'Mahoney travelled extensively after leaving the army, and in the early 1990s he worked providing security at nightclubs in London and Essex. He wrote about his experience of the violence, drugs and gang warfare associated with the nightclub culture in *Essex Boys*

Mick McGovern worked on Fleet Street before joining Thames Television's *This Week*, which he left to become a writer. His first book as co-author was *Killing Rage*, the autobiography of former IRA supergrass Eamon Collins. He work has been published in the *Observer* and *New Statesman*.

Soldier of the Queen

The only wealth in this world is our children.
I dedicate this book to my children,
Adrian, Vinney and Karis;
my brothers children,
Adam, Amy, Finn and Natalie.
To your children and our children's children.
They are our future, give them love and hope;
we can only reap what we sow.

BERNARD O'MAHONEY

with MICK McGOVERN

SOLDIER
OF THE
QUEEN

A Brandon Paperback

First published in 2000 by Brandon
This paperback edition published in 2001 by Brandon
an imprint of Mount Eagle Publications
Dingle, Co. Kerry, Ireland

British Library Cataloguing in Publication Data is
available for this book.

ISBN 0 86322 278 1

10 9 8 7 6 5 4 3 2 1

Cover design: PCC, Dublin and id communications, Tralee, Co. Kerry
Front cover photograph: Michael Abrahams, Network Photographers
Typesetting: Red Barn Publishing, Skeagh, Skibbereen
Printed by The Guernsey Press, Channel Islands

Contents

1

Home Is where the Squaddies Are

THE PORTAKABIN door crashed open and the lights flashed on. A voice shouted: "QRF! QRF! Heli-pad now!"

Bunk-beds creaked in unison as I and the other uniformed soldiers sprang to life from our half-sleep. As part of that night's QRF – Quick Reaction Force – we had to be on the helicopter and away within three minutes of getting the call. We rarely knew where we were going until we were airborne. All we ever knew for sure was that someone somewhere urgently needed our help. And in Northern Ireland's so-called Bandit Country with republican prisoners dying on hunger strike we always expected the worst – a mortar attack, a riot, a bloodied body dumped at the side of a road.

I grabbed my Self-Loading Rifle and used its strap to lash it to my wrist. That was something all of us did to stop people snatching weapons from our grasp and turning them against us in the pell-mell of our frequent violent confrontations. It was the early hours of 9 July 1981 at our base on a disused airfield near Enniskillen in County Fermanagh. Another IRA hunger striker, Joe McDonnell, had died the previous day after 61 days of fasting. He had been the fifth to die. Our local Member of Parliament, Bobby Sands, had been the first. His death two months earlier had caused much celebration at the base – exaggerated, I felt, by the need to hide the fear of what might be coming our way in revenge. Pictures of Sands still festooned the camp: juxtaposed mockingly beside them were adverts for slimming products and headlines from articles celebrating the achievements of Weight Watchers ("I lost four stone in three months"). The most popular headline was: "Slimmer of the Year".

I ran to the helicopter pad where a Lynx was waiting, rotors spinning, ready to fly us into the unknown. Fear and excitement mingled within me as I jumped in. The pilot's face looked tense as he glanced back at us. A few others had got there before me; the rest jumped in behind me. The Lynx lifted off, its nose dipping before banking away into the darkness. I was close to the pilot, who was shouting into his headset above the roar of the rotors, telling our section commander where we were going and why. I could make out that soldiers at a vehicle checkpoint (VCP) had had contact with a gunman and had radioed for assistance. I heard the words "Cassidy's Cross" and knew where we were heading. Earlier in the week our regiment had built a permanent checkpoint at a crossroads near Kinawley on the road to

Enniskillen. It consisted of four bunkers, three made from concrete and one from sandbags. However, slap in the middle was the family home of Mr and Mrs Cassidy and their two young children. The control point was in the centre, directly in front of the house; a security gate had been installed next to it to slow traffic travelling towards the nearby border with the Irish Republic. Not surprisingly, the family had not stopped complaining since our regiment's arrival: they felt they were prisoners in their own home and also feared finding themselves in the crossfire during an IRA attack. They had hardly got any sleep since we had become their unwelcome neighbours. Their days and nights were filled with the noise of soldiers shouting and car doors slamming. Disgruntled drivers added to the cacophony by complaining loudly about their treatment and sounding their horns in anger. The obvious place to site the checkpoint had been further up the road near a customs caravan in a lay-by. But customs officers had told the army to get lost: they weren't prepared to work alongside us in case they too became targets. Customs had clout, whereas the Cassidys had none. Senior officers had expressed regret to Mr Cassidy about the inconvenience. But my friends, the squaddies on the ground, had told him he could fuck off if he didn't like it. We thought that people who complained about us were certainly IRA sympathisers and quite possibly active terrorists. We would punish their Fenian cheek by using our talent for malicious mischief to upset them whenever possible.

The pilot passed on more information. A soldier in one of the bunkers had claimed he had seen a man with a gun on the hilltop facing the VCP. Soldiers had fired flares to illuminate the gunman's position; sniffer dogs were on their way. The

Lynx dipped down and landed in a field next to the VCP. We jumped out and took up defensive positions. The Lynx hovered momentarily and flew off as we set off apprehensively towards the checkpoint. As soon as we got there we knew we had nothing to fear. The squaddies were relaxed and smirking. I said to one: "This is a fucking get up, isn't it?" He smiled and nodded towards the house. He said the Cassidy children had not seen fireworks before, so they'd decided to treat them. I said: "You bastards! I was kipping." I looked up and saw the Cassidy family watching us from a bedroom window, fear on their faces. Another helicopter thundered overhead, its searchlight illuminating them as it sought the imaginary gunman. The sniffer dogs arrived, yapping and barking as they dragged their handlers up the hill looking for the same. After an hour of pointless activity the area was declared safe and the Lynx descended to take us back to base.

Three days later I found myself running towards the Lynx and heading off once again with the Quick Reaction Force to Cassidy's Cross. Earlier in the day – the twelfth of July – the large Ulster Protestant contingent in our regiment – the first of the British Army's so-called Irish regiments to be sent to Northern Ireland during the Troubles – had been celebrating their ancestors' victory over the Catholics at the battle of the Boyne in 1690, an event that seemed fresh in their minds despite the passage of the centuries. By this time the VCP had become a regimental joke. Soldiers would say to one another: "Cassidy's Cross. He's very, very cross." We were relaxed and thought we were just responding to another bit of mischief for the Cassidy family. It was after 11 p.m. and as the helicopter approached the VCP I could see a large number of headlights there. As the Lynx hovered before landing I saw a crowd of people standing in the road. My instinct for imminent violence told me there was going to be trouble. We jumped out and moved swiftly to the VCP. About 30 soldiers and policemen faced a crowd of about 150 people. I asked a squaddie what was happening. He said they had delayed one driver because they hadn't liked his attitude; then two other drivers had abandoned their cars in protest at this harassment. Suddenly about 50 other cars had come from all directions. Their drivers and passengers had all got out, blocking the road. Now they all stood staring at us with sullen hatred. The squaddie I was talking to said: "If they try to rush us I'm just gonna start shooting the fuckers."

The crowd became noisier as people started shouting insults. There had been a huge build-up of resentment at the siting of the checkpoint. Usually motorists kept their mouths shut when stopped at checkpoints. But a lot of the locals had made a point of complaining about what we were putting the Cassidys through. Such expressions of neighbourly concern usually led to the perpetrators being delayed while squaddies inspected their cars' every nut and bolt. This procedure would be done in a leisurely manner calculated to leave Her Majesty's reluctant citizens stewing with rage.

A few known republicans were spotted among the increasingly animated and vocal crowd. I had the feeling that every second was taking us closer towards violence. It just needed a spark for everything to go boom – and that was not long in coming. Our senior officer asked the police to remove the first three cars. We stood behind the police as they moved forward, backing them up. As the police approached the cars and tried to open their doors, a cry went up from the crowd. People surged towards us, shouting and screaming, expressing a rage that had been building for some time. The police had their batons out and began battering all round them. I felt that familiar adrenaline rush as I prepared to do whatever was necessary to protect myself. We began whacking everyone and anyone with batons, boots, fists and rifle butts. A long-haired man in his twenties was urging the crowd on. I heard him shouting: "Kill the fucking Brits!" To me he was a rabble-rousing bastard and I wanted to get him: I had spent months living in fear of an unseen enemy, but now in that moment I could see him. I abandoned all restraint as I moved towards him: I headbutted a face that loomed up at me and punched another before I got to my target. I grabbed him by his long hair and swung him round with such force that he fell to the ground. Another soldier kicked him in the face, while another smashed his rifle butt into the back of his head. He lay stationary on the ground, blood pouring down his face and neck.

Most of the crowd had already fallen back by this point, so a lot of people witnessed the hammering we dished out. Their anger brought them surging forward again. They threw missiles and tried to force us back down the road. We were heavily outnumbered and I thought we might be overwhelmed. I had visions of being hacked to death; I really thought one or more of us would be killed. For the first time since arriving at the VCP I experienced a feeling of real fear. However, my awareness of my willingness to kill gave me strength: if I was going to die, I had no intention of dying alone. I knew if I felt I was about to be overwhelmed I'd just start shooting. I thought that, even if I ended up being done for murder or manslaughter, a few years in an English prison would still be preferable to an early death. Someone shouted a warning and then I heard the crack of a plastic bullet being fired. The crowd fell back immediately. Suddenly it was all over – the fight had gone out of them. As we regained control I could see several people lying face down on the side of the road. Two civilians had to be taken to hospital; two policemen had also been injured. The police arrested four protesters.

We flew back to base, subdued and shaken. We all had difficulty sleeping. The incident seemed to typify our experience in Northern Ireland: one minute all was quiet, the next minute something blew up in our faces. We knew we would be facing something like that again before long. We also knew that next time we mightn't escape so unscathed.

The next edition of the local newspaper, *The Fermanagh Herald*, described what had happened as "The battle of Cassidy's Cross . . . the most serious of any checkpoint incident in the Fermanagh area for a long time." The local Irish Independence Party councillor Patrick McCaffrey was quoted describing the security forces' manner as "threatening and menacing". He said: "It was the Twelfth of July and it appears that the Orange blood was rushing through their veins and they decided they would teach the nationalist people of Kinawley a lesson . . . I am calling it an ambush, attempted murder. Rubber bullets were fired. I saw one man being taken to the side of the road and then made lie down. He was then kicked and the blood was spewing out of his head. I believe he was one of the ones taken to the hospital." Mr Cassidy said his children had been greatly upset by the incident and could not be consoled. The army denied firing plastic bullets. The denial made us laugh. Technically the army was telling the truth in the sense that they had accounted for all the rounds that had been officially issued, so none could therefore have been fired. However, outgoing regiments pass on "extra" rounds to incoming regiments, which means that after such incidents soldiers can usually produce all the rounds they were issued with and so can "prove" they didn't open fire.

Ten days later the army dismantled the checkpoint at Cassidy's Cross. The local paper applauded the decision: "The quickness of the Army's reaction in dealing with their case – indeed the fact they reacted at all – showed a genuine concern by the Regiment based here at present, the 5th Royal Inniskilling Dragoon Guards." I do not suppose the Cassidy family or the hospitalised protesters thought we had shown them much concern. And I know that many of the people I encountered in the name of the Queen during that violent summer of 1981 did not think I showed them any concern. But at that time I could not have cared less. To me I was in a war and they were all the enemy. The only concern I had was for myself and a handful of my fellow soldiers. I had no intention of becoming a casualty in someone else's war.

The protesters and the other nationalists I battered during our four and a half month tour of duty must have regarded me as just another vicious Brit in uniform. They might have been surprised to know that, despite my English accent, my parents were Irish Catholics – and that some of my relations lived just over the border.

I hadn't wanted to be a soldier, but I hadn't wanted to go to prison either. However, at the time I joined the army those had been the alternatives I faced. I doubt whether I was the British Army's most unlikely recruit, but I must have been in the running for that accolade.

2

Irish Born and Beaten

BEWARE THE Ides of March, they say, only bad things happen on that day.

My mother didn't know the 15th of March had ancient links with impending danger, although she did know something was up when I started kicking my way out of her womb as she did her shopping. The year was 1960 and the place was Dunstable in the English county of Bedfordshire. My mother collapsed in the street with the first contractions, then picked herself up and staggered home to our council maisonette. She sent my four-year-old brother out to summon help, but he went to play in the garden instead. So, as always, she just got on with it. Apparently – it's not one of my memories – I made my way out easy enough and emerged onto the front-room floor. My mother broke the umbilical cord with her hands and I started screaming. Perhaps I knew what was coming; perhaps I'd picked up in the womb that I was about to move into the domestic equivalent of what the army would call a hostile environment.

My mother came from Sligo town, one of 13 children raised in a four-bedroom council house. I was her third child: there were two boys before me, Jerry and Paul. I was christened Patrick Bernard, taking the first name from my father and the second from my uncle. As soon as I could exercise any choice in the matter I stopped using my father's name. He came from Dungarvan in County Waterford, but never told me anything about his background. In fact he never told me anything about anything: there was no such thing as a normal conversation in our home. Over the years I have pieced together fragments of his story and, although I'll probably never stop hating him, I have come to understand better why he became such a vicious bastard. Things started going wrong for him at birth: he was born illegitimate at a time when, and in a place where, illegitimacy stamped you with the mark of the beast. Hate the sin, but love the sinner, Christians sometimes say, but at that time in Catholic Ireland I think they must have hated the sin, the sinner and the product of the sin. The experiences of his childhood killed any decency within him and convinced him that only by suppressing any normal human emotion could he hope to survive. That was what life had taught him and it was the only lesson he wanted to pass on to his children. He hated to see us showing emotion. Even as infants he expected us to behave like grown men, or, rather, like the man he had grown into – cold, hard and ruthless.

But still those first few years in Dunstable were relatively happy – at least compared to what came later. My mother has quite fond memories of the time: going for walks on the downs, visiting nearby Whipsnade Zoo and getting money regularly from my father, who worked on the production line at the nearby Vauxhall car factory. However, for some reason when I was four he decided he wanted to move to Bilbrook, near Wolverhampton. Almost as soon as we arrived things changed for the worse. My father, who had always drunk, began to drink excessively. He also became extremely violent towards all of us, my mother especially. He would come home barely able to stand, spitting obscenities at my mother before beating her senseless and slouching off to bed. Memories of my mother screaming as she was beaten still haunt me. She would be screaming for him to stop and we the children would be screaming with fear. Other nights, even without much drink taken, he would just turn off the television and sit there slandering her family, humiliating her, degrading her, even questioning the point of her existence. His most decent act would be to send us to bed. Then I would lie awake in the darkness listening to her sobbing downstairs, pleading with him to stop. As I got older I would sometimes overcome my fear and shout out: "Leave her alone, you bastard." And he would come running up the stairs to beat me.

My father had his drinking to finance, so for our upkeep he gave my mother either no money or very little money. I hid in the front room with her when creditors came knocking. My mother took on three jobs to feed us: cleaning in the very early morning, working on a factory production line during the day and cleaning again at night. Sometimes my father would even manage to take off her the little she earned. I grew very close

21

to my mother and only felt secure when she was near. For this reason one of the most traumatic days in my life was my first day at school. I remember the pain and sadness I felt as I left her at the cast-iron railings of St Peter's and St Paul's in the centre of Wolverhampton. She was crying and I was crying. She told me to hang on to the red toy petrol-tanker she had given me. The next thing I remember is standing in a queue with the other boys. An older boy grabbed hold of my toy and said toys were not allowed. He tried to pull it off me; I pulled it back. A struggle developed and the other boys started shouting: "Fight! Fight!" A nun swooped down and separated us. She asked me my name.

"Bernard O'Mahoney," I said.

She said I had to call her "sister" whenever I spoke to her. "You're going to be trouble, aren't you, O'Mahoney?"

I said yes.

She screamed: "Yes, what?"

I said: "Yes, I am going to be trouble."

She put her hands on my shoulders and shook me: "What did I just tell you? You must call me 'sister'! You must always call me 'sister'! Do you understand?"

I can still smell the smells of that day, especially the lunchtime ones. I did not like liver, hated the smell and never ate it at home, so of course the first school meal had to be liver. I sat at the dinner table hardly able to touch anything: the smell of the liver had contaminated everything on the plate. Another nun spotted me. She came over, lectured me about the world's starving children, then force-fed me through my tears. Finally I swallowed the last revolting mouthful, then ran to the toilet and vomited up everything. When the final bell went that day I was a ball of emotion: I couldn't wait to get out of that hellish place. I ran to the gates where my mother was waiting and hurled myself into her arms. As we travelled home on the bus I felt secure once again. I prayed for the bus to keep on going and going, away and away from the school and on past the house of my bastard father.

My mother was religious, my father pretended to be. My mother acted in a Christian spirit, my father acted out the Christian rituals. Like all God-fearing Irish-Catholic families, we had that picture of the Sacred Heart of Jesus hanging above the fireplace in our front room. Even to this day I hate it. Before we went to bed my father would make us kneel before it and say our prayers out loud. He would shout and swear at us drunkenly if we had not prayed to his satisfaction. His God looked from the picture, arms open, bleeding nail wounds in his hands, a bleeding open heart and a pitiful look on his face. My brothers and I would gaze back, terrified and crying. If my father had known what my infant mind was asking of God, he might have stopped me praying, because I used to pray with all my heart that he would drop down dead. On Sundays we had to go to church, although my father rarely went himself. He would mess us about so much making sure our Sunday best looked right that we would always be running late. This would lead to violence. On the times he accompanied us he would usually stop us in the church porch, near the two bowls of holy water, and punch, prod or kick us for making him late. He would threaten to give us an even bigger beating at home if we misbehaved inside.

My father had another notion to move, this time to Codsall, a small town quite close to Wolverhampton. He had found us a three-bedroom terraced house there which backed onto the main railway line. At night I felt the house was going to fall in on us as coal trains thundered past at the end of the garden. In 1967 my youngest brother, Michael, was born prematurely and went into intensive care. Following the birth my mother became extremely ill and had to stay in hospital. Michael grew stronger, but my mother got weaker. One night my father – at my mother's insistence – took us to see her in hospital. She waved and smiled at us from behind a glass screen, but she looked so ill. I was terrified she would never come home. My father showed no concern either for my mother or for the new baby: he would not let anything interfere with his drinking. At one point we didn't see him for three days. There was no money and no food in the house. We survived on school dinners. Our local GP even called on my father and appealed to him to take better care of us, but my father ignored him. In the end my mother was so worried about us that she discharged herself from hospital.

As I grew older I didn't try to hide my hatred for my father. I forced myself to endure his violence stoically: I didn't want him to know he was hurting me. His dislike for me seemed to grow in response to my defiance. His physical violence only ended up hardening me, but his verbal violence had a more disturbing effect. He would grip me by the throat or hair, shouting obscenities in my face while prodding or punching me in the head or body. His favourite insult to me was a reference to the circumstances of my birth.

"You were born in the gutter," he would say, "and you'll die in the gutter." He would tell my brother Paul that our mother had tried to kill him by pushing him in front of a bus when he was in his pushchair: "She didn't want you, son," he would scream.

When we came in from school we had to go straight to the

small utility room where the coal was kept and clean our shoes until they shone. Then we had to take them to my father in the front room for inspection. He would check the soles for dirt and if they were not to his liking – and they never were – he would throw them back at us. If he had to do this more than once he would follow us into the utility room and stand over us while we cleaned, slapping and punching us. But this was nothing compared to what he saved for our mother. She would never spend anything on herself: she never owned a coat and her other clothes tended to come from jumble sales. She never smoked, drank or even went out socially. Yet he treated her like a dog. In fact, if she had been a dog he would probably have been arrested for cruelty, but because she was his wife the police and others felt there was nothing they could do. It was, they said, a domestic.

There was only one neighbour, Peggy – by coincidence a woman we had known in Dunstable – who would stand up to my father. Peggy told him to his face that he was a pig. She could see through the charade of "good old Paddy" he would put on for his drinking buddies. He was wary of her and told my mother to keep away from her.

One Mother's Day I brought my mother home a card that I had made at school. She put it on the sill above the kitchen sink. I was still sitting at the table eating my dinner when my father came home smelling of drink. My mother was still at the sink. He saw the card and picked it up.

"Is this what your little pet got you, is it? Mother's little fucking pet." My mother asked him to stop, but that only made him worse. He turned to her and said: "Shall I give you something for Mother's Day, shall I?" He picked up a plate off the draining board and went to smash it over her head. She

25

raised her arm to protect herself and the plate broke across it, cutting it wide open. She spent the rest of Mother's Day in casualty getting it stitched. Another evening he came home and complained that his dinner was not freshly cooked, just heated up. Presumably he expected my mother to guess what time he would stagger back from the pub. He threw the dinner and the plate against the wall, grabbed my mother by the hair and started punching her. She was bleeding from the nose and mouth but he kept punching her until she collapsed on the floor. He stood over her, big fucking man, as she lay on the floor, his hands and shirt smeared with her blood. My mother raised her head slightly, coughed up some blood and asked me to get her some water. My father said he would get it. He walked out of the room and I helped my mother to sit up. He came back holding a mug of water: "Here Anna. You wanted fucking water – take it." And with that he dashed the mug into her face.

I used to go to school in the mornings like a bomb waiting to explode. I loathed the other children's happiness: "Daddy did this for me, daddy did that for me." I needed to shut them up. I used to fight them with a ferocity fuelled by a hatred of their normality and happiness. Even at that young age I was developing a fearsome reputation for violence. I must have spent more time in front of the headmaster than in lessons. When those in authority were standing there shouting at me I would take myself to another place in my mind, re-living a favourite film or a great football moment. My apparently cold and detached manner would infuriate them more and I would usually end up being physically shaken out of my daydreams. I was not invited to another child's house until I was ten, when I went to the birthday party of my next-door neighbour,

Nicky. There were about 12 children there, as well as adults, and everyone was laughing and joking. Their joy made me feel angry and down. One of Nicky's presents was a model of an American Flying Fortress bomber. When all the other children went out to play football, I stayed behind and smashed the plane to pieces, dropping the remains behind the television.

In 1971, when I was eleven, my father decided to show me how to do up a tie. He made me stand still with my hands by my side. This meant I could only see his hands and not what he was doing with the tie. Then he undid the tie and told me to do it. I got it wrong. He grabbed the tie which was round my neck and began pulling me about with it, slapping me round the head and saying I was fucking stupid. Finally I could take no more. I shouted at him: "I wish you were fucking dead," then I punched him on the side of the head before running out of the room and up the stairs. He ran out and caught me halfway up. He laid into me with a vicious fury. I ended up at the foot of the stairs curled into a ball to protect myself from his kicks which were aimed at the small of my back. I thought he was going to kill me. My mother was screaming at him to stop. Suddenly I felt a sharp pain and my legs went numb. I began shouting: "I can't feel my legs! I can't feel my legs!" Only then did he stop. He tried to get me to my feet, but I kept collapsing. My mother ran out to call an ambulance.

As I lay on the floor waiting for the ambulance my father knelt down beside me. He pulled my head up by the hair and said: "Say you were playing and you fell down the stairs on your own or I'll fuckin' kill ye." And that is what I told anyone who asked. Fortunately, nothing was broken, but the discs in my spine were damaged in a way that even today causes me pain.

I started going to Codsall Comprehensive, a school of around 1,500 pupils. I would have fights with other boys almost every day of the week. If I came home with a black eye or another mark on me my father would beat me and offer me the only bit of fatherly advice he ever gave any of us: "Don't let people get away with hitting you. If they're bigger than you, hit them with something." We all started following his advice. My brother Paul got into a fight on a pub car park with a gang from another part of town. He ran at them with two screwdrivers, one in each hand. He stabbed three people before being beaten to a mess. He served two years in borstal. The eldest, Jerry, took on a group of men in a pub. He had armed himself with a pair of large mechanic's spanners and started clubbing all round him. The police arrived and he clubbed one of them too before being overpowered. He had given one of the men a fractured skull; a policeman had a shattered knee. Jerry was sent to prison. All of us, under my father's tutoring, had developed a capacity for extreme and awful violence. It set us apart – and set us against the world, especially the world of authority. I hardly needed to consult a fortune-teller to know where I was heading.

3

Out of Control

I NEVER felt English growing up, although I suppose I never felt properly Irish either. To be honest, with everything else that was going on, I didn't spend much time agonising about that aspect of my identity.

I knew my roots were in Ireland and I felt comfortable around Irish people. In a sense I lived in an Irish world, although there was no flag-waving Paddiness. I spent every summer holiday in Ireland, and I loved being there, especially with my mother's family in Sligo. My maternal grandfather, Tom, held republican views. He used to find my English Midlands accent comical and was always saying jokingly: "Oh, you Englishman." My older cousins seemed to spend a lot of their time playing cards in people's back gardens and by a weighbridge in the middle of the town. I remember the police turning up once to raid a game, having hidden themselves in the back of a removal van. I could not understand why they had gone to so much trouble over a group of men playing cards. I got on very well with everyone and liked the town and their way of life.

My stays in my father's hometown of Dungarvan were less enjoyable. People behaved as if a black cloud had descended on the place when my father arrived. He was well known, but not well liked. From his early years he had earned a reputation for violence and you could watch people steering clear of him. When there I would try to find out more about my father, but even the relations with whom we stayed didn't seem too sure about him. Or perhaps they were just not willing to tell me anything: he was not a subject that anyone liked talking about. All I knew for sure was that he didn't go to his mother's funeral. On that side of the family was a cousin who served a prison sentence for rioting in Belfast in the early seventies. On his release he came to live with us in Codsall for six months.

I was eleven when Bloody Sunday took place in Derry, but I can't remember the event having much of an impact on my life. My one clear memory comes from watching television and seeing a priest crouching over one of the victims, waving a blood-stained handkerchief. However, I didn't really understand what was going on. In fact the first time the Troubles registered with me was when the soldier son of a family that lived in our street got shot in Derry. IRA gunmen used a church porch to launch an attack on a Royal Horse Artillery checkpoint in March 1974. They killed one soldier and wounded two others, including my one-time neighbour, David Nuttall, whose brother Robert went to my school. The

news caused great shock and excitement in our street and I
remember a ripple of anti-Irish feeling. Around this time I had
a slanging match in the street with some of the Nuttalls.
During this confrontation I started shouting, "Up the IRA!",
presumably to wind them up, because I can't remember being
especially supportive of the Provos or even very aware of what
they stood for. However, I met David Nuttall in a pub recently
and he remembered me as being far more pro-IRA than I
remember myself. He told me that, apart from the slanging
match, I had also thrown stones at him while he was
recovering from his injuries and shouted, "You British Army
bastard!" I suppose my gut instincts were certainly pro-
republican, although I can't say I had any real political
consciousness. I tended to sympathise with anyone who fought
authority, so people who threw petrol bombs at the police and
army seemed like my sort of people.

I gradually became more aware of what has happening in
Northern Ireland, although events there still remained on the
margins of my mind. Once when I was 14 my father found
me a job in a Waterford glass factory. He was going to leave me
there as he thought a job was of more use to me than days
wasted at school. Fortunately, my mother did not approve of
the idea and she managed eventually to persuade him to take
me back to England. It was during that holiday that someone
at a Dungarvan disco reminded me forcefully of my perceived
Englishness. One of the local teenagers must have assumed I
was an ordinary English holidaymaker. Unburdened by notions
of Irish hospitality, he ambushed me in the toilets, punching
me on the nose and calling me an English bastard. He hadn't
realised I was at the disco with a mob of my Irish cousins. We
gave him and his mates a good beating outside, although my

own nose was broken. This attack did not destabilise my sense of identity: I didn't feel more English and less Irish as a result. If anything – and perhaps this indicates my essentially pro-republican feelings at the time – I sympathised with his attitude. I didn't take his attack personally: I thought it was natural for an Irishman to want to punch an Englishman.

Back home in England the intensity of violence I was prepared to unleash upon others had given me a reputation as a fighter. I started getting special treatment at school from the teachers. Most of them were wary of me, either trying to appease me by letting me away with things or else going in hard immediately. Both approaches usually led to the issuing of threats and ultimatums. I felt I had to fight their authority: I saw their treatment of me as an extension of my father's treatment. They all said I was disruptive, I was violent, I was bad, but no-one bothered to ask why. At times I would feel almost overwhelmed by a sense of hopelessness. When I look back now I think that my fighting against authority was a way of preventing myself breaking down and succumbing to that hopelessness. I had no sense of justice, no sense of right and wrong. It was me versus my father, me versus the teachers and, before long, it was me versus the police.

The cause of my first criminal conviction was laughable. I had developed a passion for Manchester United and most Saturdays I would travel around the country to watch them play. One Saturday I was with my friend, Mickey, on a train going to Bristol. We stopped at one station where there was a small group of Manchester City supporters on the opposite platform. They started jeering and shouting insults and we responded in kind. Nobody took it seriously: it was all quite light-hearted, just kids having a laugh. There was certainly not going to be a fight, if only because our train was about to move off. Once the train got going two middle-aged men in suits who had been sitting opposite us stood up and said they were British Transport Police. They said we were under arrest for using obscene language in a public place. They made Mickey and me stand in the corridor: they stood on either side of us, guarding the dangerous felons. They took us to a Bristol police station where a fat-faced desk sergeant formally charged us with using the f-word and gave us a date to appear at Bristol Magistrates' Court. Then the sergeant – his fat face bloated further with glee – told us he was not going to release us until after the match had started. He said – presumably unaware of the irony: "Don't think you little fuckers can come to Bristol and cause fucking trouble."

To top everything, my father, the man who had taught me from the cradle all the bad language I knew, had to accompany me to court. My mother had an appointment at the hospital, so he reluctantly took me. On the train journey he made three brief points: one, he had lost a day's work because of me; two, I was an ungrateful little bastard; and three, I would fucking pay for it. I stood in that court feeling bewildered, confused and angry. The magistrate gave me a lecture about bad language and fined me £5. This was my first experience of the state's justice – and it seemed no more justifiable than my father's. On the journey back my father slapped my face and punched me in the head. He told me that the money I earned from my two jobs – doing a paper round and helping the milkman – would pay for the fine and the expenses he had incurred that day.

My second criminal conviction was for an even more serious crime. At Christmas I would earn a little extra money by working at a local turkey farm. At first I did various menial jobs, but the boss soon promoted me to chief executioner – no other boy had the stomach for such grisly work. I had to put the squawking creatures head-first into a cone-shaped metal bucket; then I had to pull their heads through the hole at the bottom, trapping their necks between two metal bars; I would then simultaneously squeeze and pull down the bars, breaking their necks and killing them instantly. I think it's what they call a humane method. The birds would kick and scratch at the bucket as they fought for their lives, struggling with such force that the bars and my hands would shake. I used to close my eyes and imagine I was squeezing the life out of whoever had upset me that day, usually my father.

One evening, about a week before Christmas, I found a wrist-watch on the floor in the yard. It was useless – one hand was missing – and I assumed someone had thrown it away. When I got home that evening I gave it to my brother Paul to tinker with, then I changed and went to play football at the nearby sports hall. Later as I was playing football a policeman burst into the hall, marched up to me and said I was under arrest. I found out later that Paul had been outside a shop with his friends when the policeman had walked by and told them it was time they moved on. Paul had said something cheeky like: "No, it's about eight o'clock actually." All the boys laughed. The policeman asked him if he was trying to be funny. He said he was not: it was just that his watch only had one hand. He showed it to the policeman who asked him why he had such a useless watch. Paul said that I had found it at work and given it to him earlier. The policeman asked where I was and Paul told him. Hence, his dramatic arrival at the sports hall.

I was completely embarrassed and bewildered when in front of my friends he put my arm behind my back and frog-marched me to his van. He put me in the front seat beside him. As we drove towards the police station he kept asking me where I had got the watch and I kept telling him the truth. He shouted that I was a liar, then slapped me in the mouth with his glove. I felt frightened because I did not know what I had done to justify this treatment. I leant over and grabbed the steering wheel, forcing him to slam on the brakes. The van skidded and struck the kerb before stopping. He hit me a few times while I shouted that I wasn't going to the police station without my mother. Eventually he agreed and drove to my house. He picked up my mother and drove to the station where I was charged with "theft by finding". At court a magistrate gave me another lecture on morality and fined me £35.

Before I encountered the police I was already hurtling downwards, but far from diverting me to safety, their ludicrous petty-mindedness helped turn my descent into a kamikaze nose-dive. In my adolescent mind all I could see was that the forces of law and order could hound a boy for petty irrelevancies, but could not intervene to prevent a man from nearly killing his wife. Rage and resentment stewed inside me: school was a farce, the law was a farce, life was a farce, but I was not going to take their shit. Unlike my mother, I was going to hit back.

One evening I was walking home from school with a group of seven others. The school coach stopped at a set of traffic lights. It contained around 50 children who lived in outlying areas. They started making faces at us. We all picked up handfuls of dirt and threw them at the coach as it set off. One of us must have picked up a stone in the dirt because the coach's back window suddenly disintegrated. The next day the headmaster gathered together the children who had been on the coach. He gave them each a piece of paper and told them to write down the name of the person they thought had smashed the window: their anonymity would be guaranteed. Almost everyone wrote down my name. On that basis alone I was found guilty and ordered to pay the £100 cost of replacing the window.

I was enraged: no-one knew, or could have known, who had broken the window. I said I wouldn't pay and walked out of the school. Later that day a truancy officer called and told my father to bring me into school the next day for a meeting with the headmaster. At that meeting I explained that eight boys had thrown dirt at the coach and none of us knew whose handful had contained the stone; surely as we were all in the wrong the cost ought to be divided equally between us? Furthermore, how could most of the children – who were not even looking out of the coach window at the time – know for sure who had thrown the stone? My father told me to be quiet, apologised to the headmaster for my behaviour and said that of course I would pay the full cost. They agreed I would pay so much a week. So for 14 weeks I had to hand over everything I earned from my two jobs. I despised them and I despised their justice, just as I despised the woman who would slide back the hatch at the school office and take my hard-earned money. For the first six weeks she said the same thing: "Oh, you ought to be putting this in the bank, O'Mahoney. Maybe next time you'll think before you act. Do you want a receipt?" Then she would smile sarcastically as she slammed the hatch shut. I could imagine the poisonous bitch going home to her slipper-wearing husband and the two of them laughing at her reports of her witticisms.

One night I crept into the school grounds and hurled a crate of empty milk bottles through the headmaster's window. Then I sprayed blue paint over the school coach. I was not caught and I never told anyone I was responsible. But for the next eight weeks as I handed over my money I said to the woman: "Have they caught anyone yet?" She would say: "No, O'Mahoney. But we will. We will."

I carried out my first street robbery when I was around 13. One afternoon I was in Wolverhampton with a friend called Hughie. I saw a well-dressed boy, perhaps two years older than us, standing by a Mercedes in a back street near the town centre. He was carrying a bag containing the kit for a large model aeroplane. I did not say anything to Hughie, but we both instinctively knew we were going to rob him. I went up to him and asked if he had any money. He looked at me, laughed and in a well-spoken voice said: "Piss off, sonny." With that he pushed me in the chest and I fell backwards into a puddle. I felt gripped by a rage: I jumped up, ran towards him and started punching him in the head, face and kidneys. I spun him around so he was facing the car – it was probably his parents' and he was waiting for them to finish their shopping. I grabbed his hair and smashed his face into the bonnet. I pulled him round to the middle-centre of the bonnet and brought his head down repeatedly onto the Mercedes badge, which soon became flattened and spattered with blood. Hughie was shouting at me to stop and eventually he pulled me off. The boy collapsed limply and his body began to jerk violently. He started writhing on the floor in convulsions. I had the terrifying feeling I was watching someone's death throes. We ran to the bus stop and waited nervously for our bus. We were both panicking and I kept asking Hughie if he had seen the boy moving or breathing as we ran. He kept saying: "He'll be all right. He'll be all right." When I got home I turned on the radio to listen to the local news. Nothing. Then I went out and bought the local evening paper, the *Wolverhampton Express and Star*. Nothing. I was sure I had killed the boy, but over the next few days there were no reports of the attack, so after a while I relaxed. I can only assume now that my victim must have suffered an epileptic fit. I feel revolted, truly revolted, remembering this attack. My upbringing did not justify that behaviour and only partially explains it. I had been turned – but was also for my own dark reasons choosing to turn myself – into a cold and violent thug.

I was always fighting at secondary school, at least for the first few years when there remained people willing to take me on. The teachers tried increasingly drastic methods to lessen my disruptive influence. For a long while I was prohibited from mixing with the other children. At the end of a lesson I had to wait until my fellow pupils had made their way to the next class before I could set off after them along the empty corridors; at breaktime I had to stand alone outside the headmaster's office; at lunchtime I had to leave the premises altogether.

Not that that stopped me from forming my own gang and diversifying into illegal money-making ventures. One was the sale of alcohol from a loft in the school cloakroom. Boys would steal alcohol from home or local shops and sell it to me for cash. I would then sell it on at a profit. The other was a "steal-to-order" shoplifting scam: some pupils' parents would ask me to get them perfume or after-shave to give as presents – one even ordered a lawn-mower from me. So I employed two of my fellow pupils, both competent shoplifters, to get what they wanted for a price. Both scams added to my income, helping to pay my fines while funding my weekly trips to watch Manchester United.

At school I would also use whatever opportunity presented itself to get back at teachers I didn't like. In one chemistry lesson I handed the teacher a test-tube whose top I'd heated over a Bunsen burner. The unsuspecting teacher grasped it in his palm and screamed in agony as the tube attached itself to him, burning its way into his skin. He shook his hand violently to shake off the tube, but it had stuck to his palm. The chemical reaction caused by hot tube combining with hand was still hissing and smoking as the teacher ran screaming from the room.

My best friend at the time was Stan, the son of a policeman. He had been present at my first attempted burglary when I had broken the catch on a local supermarket's store-room window in the hope of gaining access. However, we couldn't get inside and had to be content with reaching in and grabbing what we could – Jaffa Cakes and whisky. Stan was also having problems at home, although these were completely unlike mine. He did not like his step-mother and felt she did not like him. He told me she seemed to care less about him than she did about "Chuckles" – her Pekinese dog with its short legs, broad flat face and long shaggy coat. One day I was in his front room when his step-mother walked in. She ignored us and walked out again. We heard her shout: "Chuckles! Chuckles! Come on!" Chuckles was laid out on a cushion in front of the coal fire. It failed to respond to its mistress's call. She kept calling but must have decided to leave without the dog, because we heard her slam the back door shut. The noise woke up Chuckles, who jumped up and made as if to go out. Stan gave the dog a half-hearted kick which, to our horror, projected Chuckles into the blazing fire. Chuckles's coat appeared to explode into flames. The dog jumped off the fire and ran around the room barking, chased by the two of us who were desperately trying to extinguish the flames. The more we chased Chuckles, the more it panicked: it ran behind the full-length curtains and they too caught fire. Eventually we managed to catch poor Chuckles and smother the flames. We had put out the fire on the curtains immediately, so there was not too much damage there. Chuckles was shocked, but once we had cut off most of the singed and burnt hair, the poor dog looked like a passable imitation of its old self. Thankfully the fire had looked worse than it was: the perfumed scent that Stan's step-mother sprayed on the dog had probably ignited to give a look of fiery intensity, without causing real burning heat. We arranged the curtains in such a way that at a glance you wouldn't have noticed the fire damage. Then we sprayed air freshener to mask the acrid smell of burnt hair. Stan's step-mother never did find out what had happened that day. She saw the burnt curtains, found a burn on the carpet and could tell by Chuckles' new look that something had happened, but Stan, as always, denied knowing anything.

Stan and I got into all sorts of trouble, much to his policeman father's despair. One time we ran away from home to Wales where we ended up in court charged with theft. We were given a 12-month Supervision Order. This experience did not stop us: we kept breaking in to the supermarket from which we had stolen the Jaffa Cakes and whisky some time before. We never got away with much. However, one night we were spotted and someone called the police. We split up as we ran off. I got away, but Stan ended up being caught by his own father, who was on duty. His father – the most decent policeman I have ever known – had to arrest him and take him to the police station. None of us, including his father, thought Stan would be punished too severely, even though he had a previous conviction. However, to everyone's shock, he got sent to a detention centre. But my friend's imprisonment didn't deter me – it just made me loathe authority even more.

No-one ever seemed to question why I was so unruly. No-one witnessed the physical and mental torture I endured at my father's hands. I was just "bad" and had to be punished. But the special treatment I received and my reputation for violence gained me what I thought was the respect of my peers. In fact, it was only deference based on fear. But I liked it. It made me feel powerful – an enjoyable sensation for someone who had felt powerless for so long. People could only see this aggressive couldn't-care-less delinquent; they could not see the confused and frightened child I knew myself to be. I wish I could have broken and poured everything out to someone. Instead, I continued to act out my bad-boy role, because at least that way I could get a bit of adoration and recognition, which is what I craved. I soaked up the attention of my minions. In my mind I felt I was beginning to win the fight against those who tried to impose their authority on me. I thought I was becoming a somebody – a status they had said I would never achieve. In reality I was systematically destroying myself and my future.

At home, throughout my early teens, I would harm myself, gouging my stomach with a craft knife or broken glass. I did not want to feel I was being hurt by my father and when I realised I was I hated my weakness and wanted to harm myself: emotion and pain were for weak people. I had learnt that from my father and he frequently underlined the point: once when I was about 13 I accidentally cut my hand wide open with a knife while playing. I ran into the house crying with pain. My father looked at me with contempt and said: "What you fucking moaning about? Put your hand here and I'll fucking stitch it." And he did: he got a needle and thread and stitched it. As I moved into my teens my father continued to use me as a punchbag, so I used to try to avoid him. I would sit on the pavement outside the house some nights waiting for every light to go out. When I thought he was asleep I would slip in quietly by the back door and go silently to bed.

In November 1974, four months before my 15th birthday, the IRA blew up two pubs in nearby Birmingham, killing 19 people and injuring 182. My brother Paul was one of many employed to clear up the wreckage. The bombing caused an outpouring of anti-Irish feeling throughout the country, but especially in the West Midlands. We all felt it: my father was attacked at the Wolverhampton tyre factory where he worked. Unfortunately, he was not badly hurt. My mother found people ignoring her in the shops and giving her dirty looks in the street. Even today when something dramatic happens in Northern Ireland she doesn't like leaving the house.

The bombing became an issue for me at school when I got into an argument with my history teacher. We were studying the Second World War and the teacher made a comparison between the brave RAF pilots who flew bombing missions over Germany and the IRA cowards who planted bombs in pubs. I said that in my opinion it did not take a lot of courage to fly over Germany in the dark and press a little button to bring death to the unseen men, women and children below. Planting a bomb in a pub, on the other hand, where you would have to look into the eyes of those around you – especially women's eyes – knowing you were going to kill every one of them required either great courage or inhuman coldness. I was not supporting what the Provos had done: it had shocked and disgusted me. In fact, it had turned me completely against the IRA – the effect it had on a lot of one-time republican sympathisers – and I hoped the perpetrators would themselves die horribly. However, for all that, I still couldn't regard them as cowards – and that was the main point I wanted to make. I suppose an underlying point was that people never looked at the atrocities committed by their side, but always rushed to condemn those committed by the enemy. But I had hardly chosen the best time to express such opinions and I caused a huge row. I felt I had made the teachers hate me even more than they already did.

Not that I cared: their opinions meant nothing to me.

4

The Fall of the Tyrant

B Y THE time I was 15 I had come to regulate myself by my own rules: laws enforced by police officers as part of what I saw as the no-justice system had become irrelevant to me. I had developed my own warped values – and my behaviour soon became even more warped.

I started getting involved in huge gang fights against rivals from other areas. Our main rivals were from a suburb of Wolverhampton called Tettenhall. Sometimes there would be as many as 200 of us battling in parks and on waste ground. When people began to get seriously hurt the police became involved and numbers dwindled to a hard core of about 30 on each side. The younger boys would pass on messages arranging the venue for the next encounter. I knew someone vaguely associated with the Tettenhall gang and sometimes he would give me advance warning of planned ambushes. He told me one evening that members of the Tettenhall gang would be at a particular disco: they planned to come looking for some of us afterwards. I decided to pre-empt them. I got a friend called Cyril to take me to the disco on his motorbike. We set off on our mission, not knowing quite what we would be up against. We walked into the darkened disco: the flashing strobe lights momentarily illuminated a group of the Tettenhall boys at the bar. They saw us at the same time. The DJ knew me and came over for a brief chat before returning to the stage. As he passed the Tettenhall boys they threw drink over him and jostled him. I knew they were hoping to provoke me into doing something. One of their number kept looking over at me, so I mouthed the word "wanker" at him. He came bowling across the dance floor and I went to meet him half-way. We had almost reached each other when I took a step back and kicked him as hard as I could between his legs. Before he had slumped to the floor the place erupted into violence. Cyril and I were fighting side by side as hard as we could, but we were completely outnumbered and I was sure we were going to get a hiding. Girls were screaming and the lights had been turned on. However, for some reason, one of their gang turned and ran; this led to a collective collapse of nerve and they all followed him. We chased them to the exit and stood by the doors to make sure they did not come back in. I could see two stewards putting onto a stretcher the boy I had kicked: he appeared to be gasping for breath. As they carried him out Cyril picked up a heavy pint glass and smashed it across the head of the outstretched patient. The stewards were too astonished to say or do anything. We just walked out of the hall and away.

A few weeks later I was walking through Tettenhall with Cyril and three others when we came across a gang of about 25 of our rivals. I knew if we ran then some of us would probably get caught and beaten. I told everyone to run at the Tettenhall gang who were about 400 yards down the road. At first they stood their ground and looked confident, but as we got closer I could see their courage fading. A few at the back turned and ran which panicked the rest: all but one of them took off up the street. I told Cyril and a boy called Des to get the remaining boy while three of us chased the stampeding herd. They had fear on their side and had got too far away for us to catch them. I ran back to find Cyril and Des fighting the solitary Tettenhall boy. Cyril was punching him in the head, while Des was trying to kick the boy's legs from under him. But he was still giving as good as he was getting. We were in a residential street and I knew someone would soon be calling the police. I had to end the fight quickly. I ran to a doorstep and picked up two empty milk bottles, then ran back and smashed one of them over the boy's head. He released his grip on Cyril and clutched his head. I smashed the other bottle over his head and he fell to the floor. I started to kick him, but he was a hard little bastard and managed to struggle to his feet and fight back. One of the terraced houses near us had been converted into a shop: its front door was one complete pane of glass. As we grappled I turned the boy so his back was towards the glass door and then with all my strength I charged him into it. With a loud crash he went straight through and lay sprawled on the floor, not moving. I picked up a metal "Paraffin Sold Here" sign and threw it on top of him. Then we ran off.

My passion for Manchester United grew to the point where I used to live for Saturdays when I would follow the team around the country. I loved the football on the pitch, but the hooliganism off the pitch added greatly to my enjoyment. I engaged in countless running battles across the terraces or in town centres, getting high on the feelings of power and unity that came from taking part in mob violence. I remember once there were about 1,000 of us surrounded by police on Blackpool beach. We wanted to break out of the cordon: we started throwing bottles and then, as one, ran at the police. They hesitated for a moment before turning and running, pursued by us. The moment was captured by a photo on the front page of the local evening newspaper which was on sale at the train station by home-time.

Most of my Codsall friends supported the local team, Wolverhampton Wanderers. I would go with them to what I regarded as good games, that is, ones where trouble seemed guaranteed, such as a local derby against a team like Birmingham City. We would catch an early train to avoid the crowds and police; we wouldn't wear scarves, badges or football shirts. Anyone looking at us would have thought we were just a group of young lads on a day out. Before the game we would rob sports or clothes shops by the method known as "steaming". This would involve choosing a shop with no more than two assistants; two of us would take up their attention by posing as potential customers, then the rest would steam into the shop, fanning out and grabbing whatever they could before running out. We would stash our heist in lockers at Birmingham New Street Station – not far from the site of the pub bombs – before continuing the day's recreation by hunting down rival supporters. I loved the sounds of glass smashing, people screaming, police sirens. The uncertainty of the outcome would keep me alert and pull me violently through the scale of emotions: euphoria as the hunter, panic as the hunted, but all the time a constant flow of adrenaline. Mayhem and disorder had become the sources of my joy.

As we got older we used to carry craft knives with us – but with a vicious twist: we would put two blades in the holder, place a matchstick between them and tighten up the case. When the victim was slashed he would suffer two identical wounds only the thickness of a matchstick apart. This meant surgeons would be unable to stitch the wounds and the victim would be left with a horrible thick scar, usually across his face. On the way to a night match against Birmingham City our gang encountered a group of rival supporters and we began fighting. One of them turned to flee and was slashed across the back. The razor blades tore through his clothing, opening him up from the top of his neck through his shoulder blade to the middle of his back. He collapsed immediately, blood seeming to spurt everywhere. We ran, suddenly terrified he would bleed to death. We swapped clothing to confuse attempts to identify us and stood apart during the match. It was not the first or last time we believed we had seriously injured or even killed someone.

Another time Stan and Hughie called at my house to see if I'd go with them to a Wolves versus Chelsea game. I didn't want to go because my shoes had fallen apart. The pittance my father gave my mother barely fed us; it certainly didn't clothe us. Indeed, the only time I ever had anything decent to wear was when I had stolen stuff. Otherwise most of the clothes I owned were like rags: they came either from jumble sales or were bought with Social Security vouchers. I asked Bill, a neighbour my age, if I could borrow a pair of his. He agreed to lend me a pair of his dad's extremely unfashionable slip-on plastic "pan shiners". Stan and Hughie mocked me as we made our way to the ground.

We went first to the train station to see if we could catch any Chelsea stragglers. We saw two hanging about. We walked over to them. They were several years older than us and asked if we knew where they could get a ticket for the game. I said yes and we all walked off towards the ground. Stan, Hughie and I had not planned anything as such, but by this stage in our badness we could almost communicate telepathically. We took them across some waste ground and Stan, who was walking at the rear, picked up a piece of wood and, without saying anything, whacked one of the men across the side of the head. He collapsed to the ground, dazed but not unconscious. We made the other Chelsea fan get on his knees, then we ordered both to empty their pockets. We took their money. I noticed that the taller one was wearing a newish pair of Doctor Marten's boots. I asked him what size he took. He said: "Nines. Why?" I said that was my size and told him to take the boots off. I put them on and gave him Bill's dad's pan-shiners. Stan took the man's Harrington jacket. Then I picked up their train tickets and tore them up in front of their faces before leaving. I was a loathsome bastard and I knew it. I was satisfying the seething anger inside me by inflicting misery on others.

By the time I was 16 I was completely reckless. I didn't seem to care what I did, who I did it to or whether I got caught. Hughie, Stan and I were in Birmingham one day walking around the market area below the Bull Ring shopping centre. Stan used a public toilet, but when he came out he told us a man of about 40 had asked him if he wanted to go for a drink. We knew the man did not want to discuss Stan's academic progress. We reasoned, therefore, that if we robbed the perv he wouldn't go to the police. Stan agreed to lure the man to a place where we could jump him.

We watched as Stan and the man walked out of the toilet and into a nearby cafe. Hughie and I kept walking past the window: we could see Stan inside drinking tea and eating egg and chips. We became worried that Stan would spend all the man's money before we had a chance to rob him of it. But after a while they left the cafe and walked towards a nearby church. We followed. The man was well-built, so I armed myself with half a house-brick which I planned to hit him over the head with if he resisted. I put the brick in my coat pocket, but hoped I wouldn't have to use it. When they got to a relatively quiet area in the churchyard I walked up to the man. He stank of stale smoke and seemed to tower over me, which undermined my confidence. I took out a pound note and asked him if he could change it as I needed to telephone my parents urgently. I knew he wouldn't let down a boy in need. He took out his wallet and opened it to get at the coin pouch, giving me in the process a flash of a thick wad of notes. I had been feeling unsure, slightly panicky even, but the sight of the money bolstered my nerve. He counted the change out into my hand, then as I thanked him and handed over the note I purposely dropped it on the ground. He bent down to pick it up and I kicked him full in the face. He fell to his knees: I stood back and kicked him again, this time in the side of the head, while Hughie and Stan did the same. The man shielded himself with his hands, but did not fight back, which was just as well for him because I had the brick in my hand. Stan grabbed his wallet and we ran as the man shouted: "Help me! Help me! Help me!" Nobody took any notice: they never did.

We ran to nearby New Street Station and jumped on the first train to Wolverhampton. Once it started moving Stan took out the wallet and opened it. The thick wad of money turned out to be sheets of newspaper cut to the same size as money with three one-pound notes on top: it had certainly acted as bait for us young boys, though not perhaps in quite the way its owner had anticipated.

The next day Hughie and I skipped school and went back to look for more lucrative targets. We started following two boys who looked our own age. They began walking down a flight of stairs into the Queensway subway. I grabbed the taller of the two and told him to hand over his money or be thrown down the stairs. The boy's face was alight with terror, but he refused to give me anything. I took out a knife and said I'd stab him. He and his friend emptied their pockets and handed over a roll of money tied with an elastic band. The boy kept saying: "It's me mum's fucking gas money." We ran to the cafe in the market and counted the money: £30. We treated ourselves to egg and chips before setting off to look for other victims. We walked like predators through the maze of subways around the Bull Ring. We crossed into an open space between subway entrances and as we reached the mid-point we saw the two boys we had just mugged. They were not alone: there were three or four men with them who started running towards us when the boys pointed us out. Running was pointless: they were too close and we were going to have to fight. I quickly threw away the money. Hughie hit the man who reached us first. I tried to pull him onto the grass, near where I had thrown the money. But the other men were upon us and their punches were soon landing on our heads. It took a few seconds for me to realise they were shouting: "Police! Police! Stand still!

You're under arrest." I felt my arms being forced up my back. I glanced over at Hughie: he was in the same position. One of the detectives got out his radio and called for a car to take us to Digbeth Police Station.

The desk sergeant called us animals and said we were not fit to breathe the same air as decent people. He read us our rights and took down our details. Then we were put in separate cells. My cell had an arc of blood sprayed up the wall and the single tatty blanket stank of piss and vomit. A few hours later our mothers arrived: my brother Jerry had driven them to Birmingham. They looked distraught. We had been taken out of our cells while the desk sergeant filled in the forms for bail. He said: "Robbery – at your age! I'll tell you now – you'll be banged up for murder one day." Both our mothers were upset and angry; the journey home in the car was one of the longest drives of my life. I felt awful for upsetting my mother, but I didn't feel guilty about committing the crime, only regret at getting caught. I was sure we were going to be sent to a detention centre, but at the end of the judicial process the judge merely gave us "strict Supervision Orders". In reality, this meant that once a fortnight Hughie and I had to go to a council building where we sat in a room with other local hoodlums while waiting our turn to be called into an office and asked fatuous questions by a probation officer: "How are you? How's school? How are things at home? Are you keeping out of trouble?" I often used to wonder what they would have said if I had told them the truth: "Well, actually, I'm doing much the same as I was before – although I've cut down on the mugging." Sometimes while waiting our turn we would break into the probation officers' cars and fill them with rubbish. Occasionally the police would come and give us talks about the latest advances in crime detection. The burglars among us, in particular, found many of their tips extremely useful, but we all learned something to help make us better criminals. They even arranged for us to play football against a team of police cadets. We criminals turned up in working boots and started kicking lumps out of the cadets. The referee abandoned the match at half-time when the cadets refused to come out for the second half. We stood jeering on the pitch until they brought on a police dog and made us sit down.

At the end of the summer term of 1976 I left school with few qualifications. I was sixteen. I had little fear of, or respect for, anything or anyone. Only my father continued to have the power – physical and psychological – to turn me into a frightened little boy. But that was not going to last much longer. He could see what he had turned his sons into – and he must have known the day of vengeance was coming. In fact it came in August 1976. He came home, drunk as usual, and started beating my mother in the kitchen. My brother Paul and I were in the front room. We heard the familiar sounds. Paul looked at me and I looked at him and we both just got up and ran into the kitchen. Paul shouted at my father: "Leave her alone, you fucking bastard!" My father lurched towards Paul and punched him. Paul snapped: he grabbed my father by his hair with one hand and with the other began punching him in the face with an unstoppable ferocity. I stood and watched as Paul went berserk, punching and kicking until my father lay on the floor, his face a bloody mess. Everything went quiet; the only sound was of Paul breathing heavily from his exertion. I suppose we all expected my father to get to his feet and inflict violent punishment on us for this outrage, but he just stayed on the floor. He didn't move for a little while, then slowly pulled himself up. Paul was ready for more, and I was ready to help him, but we could all see that something had changed. The fight had gone out of my father. He did not say anything. He just slouched off to bed. As he walked past me I spat at him. He didn't respond. His face gave nothing away, but he had the air of a tyrant who knew his time had come.

The following morning my father got up for work as usual and told my mother he would meet her that afternoon outside the Marks and Spencer store in Wolverhampton. He said he was going to give her some money to buy some shopping. He left the house before Paul and I got up. In the afternoon my mother, penniless as usual, had to embarrass herself by borrowing money off a neighbour to get the bus into town. She waited for him for two hours, but he never turned up. She had to walk all the way home.

My father has not been seen since. Not by anyone. No-one knows where he went or what happened to him. He didn't take any clothes or personal effects. Rumours of his whereabouts came and went; some people on the estate even thought he'd been murdered. I don't know and I don't care. The less I think and know about him the better.

5

Full Blue Velvet Jacket

T HAT SUMMER of 1976 was a turning point in other ways. I left school and was taken on as an apprentice toolmaker. Like all the other boys, I'd been brainwashed into believing that life was not worth living if I didn't have a trade. I had to attend a tool factory in Wolverhampton for four weeks' "familiarisation" training before starting a sponsored college course. I soon discovered that familiarisation meant familiarising myself with the drudgery I could now expect for the rest of my life. I had to work in the stores department humping boxes and crates for a sum of money that would just about have bought me a pair of dirty overalls. The unions were very powerful at this time. On my first day I was confronted by a picket line, advised not to cross it and sent home. In the factory the union shop-stewards were constantly telling us not to do other people's jobs – such as sweeping up if you dropped something or replacing dirty towels in the wash room. I found this tedious and childish, and said so, which annoyed my adult "brothers", whose reasons for being seemed to hinge on the existence of clear demarcation lines between them and other brothers.

I was introduced to experienced toolmakers – men I was meant to admire and aspire to be – some of whom had worked on the same lathe in the same spot for twenty years. One old boy told me he had named "his" lathe Helen. "Oh, you're lucky! Helen's on good form today!" I began to feel as if I'd been given a life sentence with no chance of parole. I went to a Further Education college to start a toolmaking course and immediately got off to a bad start. A fat chain-smoking former sheet-metal-worker in stained clothes talked to me as if I were a dog and insisted I called him "Sir". I said I would only do so when Her Majesty had knighted him. Apart from criminal behaviour and Manchester United, my other passion was music. I admired the Beatles and I jumped at the chance to go to a concert in London by the former Beatle Paul McCartney, although it was going to mean I would have to take a Friday off. I told the sheet-metal slob of my plans and he wasn't happy. He said I didn't deserve the opportunity that had been bestowed upon me. At first I thought he was referring to the concert, but I soon realised he meant the prospect of being imprisoned in a factory on slave wages shackled to a lathe called Helen for the rest of my life. I said I was going to the concert and that I was telling him out of politeness, not asking his permission.

I returned on Monday to a rant from the slob about my impertinence. We had an exchange of views in which I may have used the f-word. He stormed off to the nearest phone and rang my company. I had to return to the factory "as a matter of urgency" to see the personnel manager. I urgently caught a bus into town and urgently browsed through a few record stores before making my way to the company headquarters for my showdown with Mr Personnel. When I arrived I was directed to a plastic chair outside his office by his ferret-faced secretary who kept looking at me sternly over her glasses. She reminded me of the secretary at school who used to take my money from behind the hatch.

After about half an hour an electronic box on her desk crackled: "Send O'Mahoney in." I walked towards his office under the now-you-are-in-for-it gaze of the secretary. On his door was an aluminium sign saying "Personnel Manager", probably produced on the lathe called Helen twenty years earlier. Inside, the floor was covered with a thick blue carpet embroidered with the company logo. A man in his fifties in a cheap blue nylon suit began telling me how lucky I was to have an apprenticeship, how 400 boys had applied for the ten jobs, how I had been set on the path towards life-long security and how I was now in serious danger of destroying that bright future. Then, relaxing a little, he began telling me how he himself had been a bit of a lad in his youth, but had then knuckled down to some hard work, which had brought him eventually to the position he now occupied. He looked at me firmly, eyes oozing sincerity, and said that with application anything was possible: "Who knows?" he said. "One day, in ten, twenty years' time, you could be sitting in this seat in this office." On the journey from the plastic chair past the aluminium sign I had made up my mind. Any lingering doubts had been quashed by the atmosphere of his crummy office: the sagging features of his miserable wife stared up at me from a photo. She seemed almost to be imploring me, "Please don't end up like the git I've married." For a few seconds I looked at him festering in his cheap suit, then I said that if I ever ended up like him I'd kill myself. In case he had not got the point I added: "You can poke your poxy job." I walked out, leaving him stumbling for words.

I soon got another job working for a scrap-metal merchant underneath Wolverhampton's railway arches. The work was hard and tedious, but I liked the people I was working with – and I was earning about five times as much as before. However, my time there ended abruptly one afternoon when the hammers on the frag machine (so called because it would pulp metal into fragments) became jammed. A fitter climbed in to free them – without shutting down the machine. He freed the hammers, but the machine then started up, pulling him into its jaws. Someone managed to press the stop button quickly, but not before the fitter's legs had been mutilated: one was almost severed, the other shattered. The Health and Safety Executive immediately shut the yard; the management laid off the work force.

I could not decide what to do with myself. I was tired of living in Codsall, tired of the same old faces haunting the same old places, saying and doing the same old things. I was living at home with my mother and my youngest brother, Michael. My oldest brother, Jerry, had moved into a house in Wolverhampton with the Hell's Angels, while the second oldest, Paul, was still in borstal serving what should have been a six-month sentence but which had been extended to two years for bad behaviour. I had made pregnant my girlfriend of three years. She gave birth to a boy, Adrian, but then dumped me. With hindsight, I know she made a wise decision, but at the time I was heart-broken. I decided to leave the area: I packed a holdall and said goodbye to my mother, not knowing where I was going or what I was going to do when I arrived there. Saying goodbye to my mother devastated me. I walked the five miles to the M6 motorway in tears. I decided to leave my final destination to fate: I would stick my thumb out and go wherever the first car to stop was going.

That night I found myself trudging in a blizzard through a run-down area of Glasgow. I slept in a tin workman's hut near the Celtic football ground and in the morning I explored the city. I had heard unemployment was high in Glasgow, but I didn't think things could be that bad. Then I found a Job Centre that appeared not to have any jobs on its boards. When I enquired at the desk the clerk started laughing. He called over his colleagues to show them the Englishman who had come to Glasgow to find work. As he sent me away he said: "You're at the wrong end of the motorway, Dick Whittington." I lived rough in Glasgow for a few days before moving on and doing the same in Edinburgh and then Dundee. I started having breakfast every morning at a particular Dundee cafe where I got talking to another regular called Derek. He said he ran a cheap hotel and he asked me if I'd like to be its caretaker-cum-porter. I said yes, but soon discovered the hotel was little more than a brothel in a rough part of town. Prostitutes hired out his rooms by the day or the week. All I had to do was answer the door, let in the punters, make sure they left and collect "room rent" off the women on Fridays. Derek just needed someone there all the time. I spent most of my day playing cards with the women or watching TV with them. All the women, without exception, were trying to escape their own traumas, only to have plunged themselves into a worse existence. After a few months the human misery I was witnessing began to depress me and I left for home.

In Codsall not much had changed. My brother Paul was home, having been released from borstal. He had worked briefly with some well-meaning nuns in London handing out soup to the homeless, but had decided against making a career of it. For some reason known only to himself he then joined the Spanish Foreign Legion. He served as a paratrooper for two years, but spent most of his time in the guard house for breaking the rules. In the end he deserted. He sneaked himself on to a British cruise liner containing holidaymakers bound for England. When the ship docked at Tilbury in Essex he was arrested by police for being a stowaway. Local magistrates showed him mercy and gave him a non-custodial sentence. He had no money when he left the court, but a reporter paid for his ticket home to Codsall and even gave him some extra cash in return for a photograph of him which then appeared in our local evening paper. During this period my brother Jerry also moved back home, although he still maintained his links with the Hell's Angels. He became obsessed with catching a rat that sometimes appeared from under the garden shed. One day I was watching a film in the front room with my mother when there was an explosion outside. I ran to the window and saw that the shed had disintegrated. Jerry came down from his room and said he'd been waiting for the rat to poke its nose out and when it had done so he had fired both barrels of a twelve-bore shotgun at it. My mother, long acquainted with the bizarre and the violent, was most concerned about the shed. Her only reference to Jerry's shotgun was her suggestion that perhaps it would be easier in the future to let the cat deal with any rats.

I stayed in Codsall for a while, but I kept getting into trouble with the police, who hated me. I was in a local pub one evening; a group of about nine men were singing rugby songs and generally being loud. They were nothing to do with me. A woman of mixed race came into the pub with her white boyfriend, who was about 30. The rugby group started singing a song which included a line about Zulu warriors. The woman's boyfriend must have assumed I was with the singers, because he came over to me and told me to tell the men to stop singing as his girlfriend was getting upset. I told him the singing was nothing to do with me. He became aggressive and said he would "do" me if the singing did not stop. I was not going to wait to get done by this man, so I hit him over the head with a cider bottle and ran out of the pub. He chased after me. I ran down someone's driveway and picked up two empty milk bottles from a step. The man lost his nerve and began walking away. I ran after him, but stopped after 100 yards. I thought the matter was closed, but the man called the police and moments later I was arrested. I was charged with assault occasioning actual bodily harm, threatening behaviour, possessing an offensive weapon and theft. "Theft? What the fuck did I steal?" I said. "Two milk bottles," said the jubilant policeman. The Codsall police had hit me with every possible offence, presumably in the cherished hope that I'd finally be sent to jail. I think they almost regarded that end as a performance-target. I was already under a two-year Supervision Order for the Birmingham mugging, so having breached that I thought there was now a good chance I'd be sent to jail at my next appearance before the magistrates. I had turned 18 some months earlier and I knew that the leniency usually extended to juvenile delinquents tended to cease sharply when they turned into adult delinquents. I was given bail and a date was set for my case to be heard.

I decided to move to Telford in Shropshire where I stayed with a friend called Chris. I started selling eggs and potatoes door-to-door from an old Transit van and was earning a reasonably good living. Chris only worked sporadically, so I started paying the rent, leaving him the money every Friday. At weekends I would take him out and buy him drinks. This arrangement existed for months, but the more I did to help him, the less he did to help himself. On top of that I felt he was becoming almost resentful of me.

One Sunday evening we went for a drink at a pub which we hadn't visited before. The locals of our own age made it clear that we were not welcome. They divided their time between glaring at us and mimicking us. I felt it was pointless waiting for the inevitable, so I punched one of them in the face. Others joined in, while Chris stood on the sidelines watching. I do not know why, and I have not seen him since to get the answer, but instead of coming to help me Chris started punching me as well. I knew I had not always been wise in my choice of company, but this was extraordinary. I got a good beating – my eye was split and someone smashed a bottle over my head. I staggered home, dazed with alcohol and violence, but through the haze I felt pure rage at Chris's treachery. I waited up all night for him, but sensibly he stayed away.

He knew I had to go to work, so I assumed he would sneak back when I was out. I decided to forgo work in order to have a chance of catching the treacherous shitbag. I hid in the laundry room, having armed myself with a bread knife from the kitchen. I was not going to stab him: I just wanted to torture and terrorise him with it before giving him a good beating. Around 10 a.m. there was a banging on the front door. I thought that either he had forgotten his keys or he was checking to see whether I was at home. Either way I had him. I ran on tiptoes to the door, bread knife in hand, whisked the door open and . . . It was the rent man. He said good morning and tried to act normally, but I could tell he was a little anxious. I put my knife-hand down and told him he had caught me in the middle of cooking. He said: "I'm glad I've caught you. You owe me nine months' rent." I said I didn't owe him anything: I had given my flatmate the rent. We chatted for a few minutes before I realised that Chris had been spending the rent money. My face must have contorted with rage, because I could see the rent man beginning to get anxious again. I said: "You better go, mate. Come back another day." He left rapidly.

I think if Chris had turned up at that moment I would probably still now be serving a life sentence for his murder. Instead, I had to be content with taking out my anger on his property. I pulled his double-bed out of his room, dragged it into the back garden, piled everything he owned on top of it and set fire to the lot. I gathered up what was mine and left, leaving open the front and back doors for would-be burglars. The bonfire raged in the garden.

It was the middle of winter. I spent a week sleeping rough in an old caravan at the side of a restaurant. A good friend called Jayne let me stay at her flat occasionally, but her boyfriend got the wrong idea, so I stuck to the caravan to save her any trouble. I have never been so cold in my life. The caravan was full of old beer crates, so there was barely room to sit down. I had no bed or blankets and had to sleep on the floor, huddled in a ball: I remember waking up one morning to find that the milk in the bottle had frozen and pushed its way out an inch to look like a red-top stalagmite. To make matters worse I lost my egg-and-potato round when my van broke down, and because I didn't have an address I couldn't get any other job.

One Saturday I met up with a known thief in Wolverhampton. It was late 1978. I had been making an effort to stay out of trouble with the police, especially as I was still on bail, but I was about to find myself led astray by a dark blue velvet jacket with huge lapels, the sort of garment Marc Bolan might have worn. This one was hanging in a shop that we were browsing through. I told the thief that I liked it. He offered to steal it for me if I paid him half its value. I agreed and waited up the road while he went shopping. He arrived back 15 minutes later with a smile on his face and the jacket in his hand. Unfortunately, he had been spotted by store detectives who had followed him to see if he was planning to go anywhere else. When they pounced I had the jacket in my hand, so I was charged with theft. I didn't need my solicitor to warn me that I was almost certainly going to jail.

The velvet-jacket case was given a date at the magistrates' court before the milk-bottle-and-assault case. Any slight hope I had of avoiding jail evaporated when I arrived at court and discovered my case was to be heard by a fearsome stipendiary magistrate with a reputation for harsh sentencing. He adjourned the case for reports, but said I had already been given every chance and warned that he had in mind to impose a custodial sentence. I walked out of court knowing my luck had run out. I was homeless, jobless and facing a prison sentence that was unlikely to enhance my future employment prospects. I walked aimlessly around Wolverhampton until, near the offices of the *Express and Star* newspaper, I saw a sign in a window saying "Join the Professionals!" It was the army recruitment office. An idea bubbled up in my mind: I didn't want to become a soldier, but I thought that if I signed up I could go back to court, wave my recruitment papers at the magistrate, be let off the sentence and then before I got anywhere near a military base I could say I had changed my mind and resign.

I congratulated myself on my cunning, then walked in to join the "Professionals". Inside the office was a shiny sergeant with a moustache. "Can I help you?" he said. I told him I was considering joining the army and wanted to know more about it. His uniformed fellow "Professionals" smiled out from posters on the walls. The sergeant had a spiel as polished as his boots: he outlined enthusiastically the exciting future that awaited me. For one demented moment I half thought that joining the army might be a good idea anyway, but I snapped out of it. He asked me if I had any criminal convictions. I said I hadn't. He said it would take six to eight weeks to process my application, but he could see no problem. Once the initial processing had been done I would be sent to St George's Barracks in nearby Sutton Coldfield. He said this was a selection centre where all recruits had to go through various written and physical tests before being chosen for a specific corps or regiment. After that I would be sent for basic training with my new regiment. I filled in some forms and asked him if he could put in writing that I had applied to join.

A few weeks later I returned to court. The magistrate told me that after considering my appalling record he had contemplated sending me to crown court for sentencing, because he only had the power to give me six months' imprisonment. Before he went on to sentence me I played what I thought was my trump card: I told him I was joining the army. He had spent his life listening to the often pathetic gambits of criminals trying to avoid punishment and he tended to treat them with contempt. However, he had the air of a man who felt that most young people – certainly all young working-class men – ought to spend their youth in the army. He asked me if I could prove my intentions. I passed the army recruitment papers to the court usher who handed them to the magistrate. While he looked at them suspiciously I said that becoming a soldier was something I'd wanted to do for a long time. He said: "You might just be saying this." He spent another short while staring at the papers in front of him before turning to me with a slight smile, as if he had had a devious brainwave. He said he intended giving me a total of six months' imprisonment, a term which would take into account the most recent offence, my previous record and the breach of my current Supervision Order (thankfully, he didn't know I was also on bail for the earlier offence which had yet to be heard). However, in the light of my good intentions he was prepared to defer sentencing for a little while. What that meant, he said, was that if I was not in the army on the day he set aside for sentencing then I would be sent to jail. However, if I was a soldier by that date he would suspend my prison sentence for two years.

I walked glumly out of court thinking my trump card had been trumped. I was faced with a dilemma: either the army for three years or prison for six months. It was coming up to Christmas and I thought of the misery of being stuck in prison with people as anti-social as I. At least in the army there would be better food, a bit of money and free time. And perhaps the moustachioed sergeant was right: it might open up other opportunities for me in the future. All in all, it seemed the least unsatisfactory alternative.

The night before I went to St George's Barracks I stayed with my mother. She was pleased I was joining the army. She had never lectured me, but I knew she had been worried about where my life seemed to be leading. I had long hair then, and she was also pleased I was going to have to get it cut.

6

Pigs, Fucking Pigs

"IF ANY of you are lying, you are going to be in serious trouble," said the serious uniformed man seriously. "SER-I-OUS TROU-BLE."

I had only been in the army for one hour and could not yet distinguish between the different ranks. I was standing in a large gym with around 100 of my fellow new recruits. The serious man's face exuded doom: "So if any of you have a criminal record that you have not yet told us about, then declare it now." Such people would be discharged immediately without being punished for having lied in their application forms. However, he said, people who had lied and did not take this opportunity to come clean would be dealt with severely when the army uncovered the truth. "And, believe me, we will find you out. Our checks are stringent. STRIN-GENT."

He walked down the line, looking into our eyes. I stared straight ahead as he plodded slowly past me. I felt uncomfortable and knew that if they did carry out any checks I'd be found out. I was still under a Supervision Order for the mugging almost two years earlier – I even had my own probation officer; I had not completed the 240 hours of community service that had been imposed some time earlier for going equipped for burglary; I had a six-month prison sentence for theft hanging over me; and I was on bail for the milk-bottle case – assault, theft, threatening behaviour, possessing an offensive weapon – which had yet to be heard. Telling the army the truth was not an option. As far as I was concerned I had nothing to lose by keeping quiet: if I confessed I would be discharged straight into prison. A few people put up their hands. One had been convicted of dangerous driving after clipping the kerb in his Mini; another had been caught shoplifting when he was 13. They were hardly infiltrators from the criminal underworld, but the serious man told them to step out of line and report to the administration office.

For the next few days we had to perform written and physical tests. Their main aim was to weed out the seriously unfit and the acutely stupid, but they were also supposed to identify aptitudes that might make you suited for a particular role. I did well in both sets of tests – and was told I might make a good tank gunner. I couldn't see how such a trade would equip me to earn a living in civilian life, but the job did have some appeal. It would mean I could travel everywhere on wheels, rather than having to blunder through countryside on foot carrying a huge backpack and a rifle. So I didn't question their assessment. In any case, I had only joined the army to avoid prison, so as long as I achieved that aim I didn't really care what I did.

I didn't have much time for most of the other recruits: many of them seemed terribly keen to make the army their life. I came across the term "army barmy" for the first time as a way of describing people who loved being soldiers and adored everything to do with soldiering. The army barmies were certainly the dominant group in this intake.

There was only one recruit I got on well with. His name was Alan and he was from Rhodesia. He was bright and amusing and had done some strange things in his life. He hated blacks, especially black Rhodesians, and followed intently the progress of the war in his homeland between the whites and the black "commie bastard terrorists". He could not understand why English people seemed to treat blacks – he called them "kaffirs" – as equals. He said that when he had first arrived in England he had taken the underground from Heathrow Airport into central London. Further down the line a black man had got on and sat in the same carriage. Alan could not believe the cheek of the man: he thought blacks were forbidden to travel in the same compartments as whites – as was the case in his own country. He got up and told the man to get out of the carriage. Not surprisingly, the man refused. So Alan pulled the communication cord to stop the train. When the guard arrived to see what was wrong Alan told him to remove "the kaffir" immediately. The conductor explained that blacks in England had the same rights as whites; and he warned Alan that people who stopped trains without proper excuse could be prosecuted. Alan spent the rest of the journey in culture shock. Alan's father was Scottish, so he had no problem getting in to the British

Army, but his intention was to get an up-to-date military training and then return home to bayonet some commie kaffirs.

The army barmies would spend most of their time asking: "What do you want to be? Which regiment do you want to be in?" Some of the more crazed ones were desperate to join the Paras. I would tell them there was no way anyone could get me to jump out of a perfectly good aeroplane unless it was going to crash. At that time I had not grasped the meaning of regiments. I just thought we were all in the army and that was that. Alan explained the regimental system and told me he was going to join his father's Scottish regiment. He suggested I went with him, but my experiences in Scotland had left me with a jaundiced view of the Scots. I said: "I ain't going in no fucking jock regiment." So he suggested – because of my Irish background – that I joined an Irish one. He added: "Then you can be a war-dodger as well." I didn't know what he meant. He explained there was a policy not to send Irish regiments to serve in Northern Ireland.

My mind had been so focussed on avoiding prison that I had not until that point properly considered the most unpleasant implication of joining the army, namely, that I might have to serve in the North. Alan's suggestion of how I could dodge the war struck me as excellent. I asked him if there was an Irish tank regiment. He said there was: it was called the 5th Royal Inniskilling Dragoon Guards. Towards the end of the selection process I was interviewed and asked which regiment I wanted to join. I told them I felt drawn to the 5th Royal Inniskilling Dragoon Guards. They asked me why. I said: "Because my parents are Irish."

From Sutton Coldfield I was sent to start my seven weeks of basic training with the Royal Armoured Corps in the

Yorkshire garrison town of Catterick. A childhood of verbal and physical abuse had prepared me well for the training regime. Indeed, some days I used to feel my childhood was being repeated as pantomime farce and, unlike most of my fellow recruits, I found a lot of the extreme behaviour extremely funny. None of the instructors ever talked normally: they barked, shouted or screamed every instruction and, perhaps through fear that you hadn't heard them, would often supplement their words with punches, slaps or kicks.

My pre-existing prejudices against Scots became intensified by my encounters with the instructors, many of whom were Scottish. There was one small-arms instructor, in particular, whom we nicknamed McPsycho. He was about 6ft 1, broad-shouldered, muscular and intimidating – a real Action Man. Even his eyes moved. He lived in a state of unceasing rage, at times even frothing at the mouth, like a rabid dog that had just had its bone stolen. You dared not commit a misdemeanour on the firing range. If your weapon jammed or you fired after he had ordered you to stop or you failed in some way to follow the correct procedure he would bear down upon you, ranting hysterically, spit falling from his mouth or bubbling on his lips. The man was a health hazard. As you lay on the ground facing the targets he would stand on your back and shout about fucking idiots who did not want to listen. Then he would say something like: "Maybe they don't want to listen because their lives are so miserable they'd sooner be dead. They'd rather be buried underground so people could walk over them." At this point he would walk on the spot on the wrongdoer's back. Then as he squeezed almost the last breath from his victim's lungs he would scream: "Is your life so fucking miserable you want to die?"

"No, corporal."

"Then listen! Fucking listen!"

He would also throw handfuls of gravel or dirt at those he thought were not paying attention. You never walked anywhere with him, you always ran. If he was not alongside you shouting insults, he would be behind you kicking your arse – especially on the forced marches. They called them marches, but you spent most of the five miles running with a full kit on your back, a sub-machine-gun in your hands – tank crews did not train with rifles – and a pair of new, ill-fitting boots on your feet that rubbed your skin raw. You would run for three miles and then be ordered to walk, but not at normal walking pace, because this was a forced walk with instructors barking, "Left, right, left, right, left, right," as you lost your rhythm and co-ordination. Then you would go back to running before arriving at an assault course which you would have to cross in groups of six carrying a telegraph pole. As I was taller than most – a lot of people in the tank regiments are quite small so they can fit into the confined tank space – I had to carry the pole on my shoulder. The smaller recruits in the middle did not have to bear so much of the weight. As I crossed the course the pole would be bouncing and smashing into my head and shoulder, giving me a red-raw shoulder to complement my red-raw feet.

The training was so intense that you were physically exhausted all the time. On a good day you would fall into bed at 11 p.m. and crawl out at 5 a.m. But you did not usually have much time to sleep, because just as you fell into blissful oblivion around 3 a.m. the doors would be flung open, the lights would be switched on and a group of psychotic Scottish instructors would be standing there screaming. You would leap six feet in the air to land at the side of your bed in your underclothes. At first some people tried to be smart by wearing their uniforms in bed to save having to change swiftly. A few punches in the head and the instructors' observation that "Only pigs wear clothes to bed" put an end to that ruse. Others would sleep on the floor so as not to have to make their beds. But the instructors knew all the tricks and they dealt with that one by dashing unexpectedly into the room, grabbing the feet of their victim and dragging him across the floor into the corridor where he would be kicked about.

As you stood to attention by your bed you would be ordered to run downstairs to play the instructors' favourite game – Changing Parades. They would order you to change into a bizarre combination of clothing which you had to wear in the stipulated order. They would say things like: "On your feet you'll have plimsolls, on your legs you'll have lightweight trousers, then your number two uniform jacket, then I want you to wear a metal helmet and your towel round your neck." Then they would shout: "Go! Go! Go!" and you would run back upstairs to change, then run back down as fast as you could. The first three downstairs would be allowed to go back to bed; the others would be ordered to change into another combination, which invariably involved wearing a gas mask. Nine times out of ten you had to keep your gas mask on for the whole exercise – sometimes running upstairs backwards – and as you got hotter and hotter you could hardly breathe, nor could you see out of the steamed-up visor.

There was one recruit who lived in dread of Changing Parades because he always ended up going to bed last. He was from south London, of slight build with short dark hair, parted at the side. Sometimes he wore glasses. He did not mix well and rarely spoke. He spent most of his time sitting alone reading war comics or books about the Waffen SS, which obsessed him. Even his civilian clothing was Second World War replica or original: brown leather USAF flying jacket with fur collar, green German paratroop trousers and Afrika Korps camouflage fatigues. Around his bed space, instead of photos of his family or pornographic posters, he had pictures of Nazi tanks. We nicknamed him Rommel. He knew everything there was to know about Waffen SS panzer divisions, especially their soldiers' clothing and weaponry. He wanted to join the Royal Tank Regiment because their tank crews were the only ones in the British Army who wore black overalls – like his SS panzer heroes. Members of other tank regiments wore green. He would also listen to tapes of the "Speak German in a Fort-night" variety, although he claimed this was because we were likely to be posted to Germany. We used to take the mickey out of him and sometimes he would play up to us, goose-stepping up and down the room with his right arm outstretched in a Nazi salute. However, although he was clearly army barmy, his military enthusiasm did not translate into military efficiency, which was why, among other things, he feared Changing Parades.

One night as we frantically changed into the latest bizarre combination of clothing he could not find a particular item and said: "Fuck. I'm going to be last again." I suggested that if he wanted to be first down he ought to jump out the window. As we were twenty feet up on the third floor I thought he would take my suggestion as the joke it was meant to be. But in his desperation it must have seemed like a good idea, because the next second he was clambering out the window. The image that remains in my mind is of him looking back at me, eyes flickering madly, as he launched himself into the air. I heard a crunch and a piercing "Aaaaarrrggghhh!" and I ran to look out. Rommel was writhing on the ground; instructors were standing over him shouting, "What are you doing? What are you doing, you silly cunt?" Miraculously he did not break any bones – although he could hardly walk – and once the instructors had established that fact they forced him to crawl back upstairs to continue the game.

Throughout this time my major anxiety was that the army's stringent checks for hidden criminals would result in my exposure. During training they often called out my name and ordered me to report somewhere. The shout "O'Mahoney! Get here now!" would send the adrenaline pumping through my veins and push into my mind the vision of a dank prison cell. I would run to my fate only to be met with the scream, "What's your doctor's name?" or some other petty administrative query. With hindsight I needn't have worried about being booted out for lying. Either they never checked my record or they decided to ignore what they found. I was not the only person to conceal his past: during my three years in the army I came across many people – at least 20 – with undisclosed criminal records, often involving crimes of violence. I only heard of one instance where they confronted someone over a discrepancy in his application. This concerned a soldier who had not mentioned his Polish relations. The Cold War was still being fought and they were worried about being infiltrated by spies from behind the Iron Curtain. But after a little hoo-ha even he was allowed to remain.

While I could tolerate, even enjoy, the physical and mental challenges of the intense training regime, there were many petty idiocies that I loathed. Supreme among these was the fetish for perfect cleanliness and order in all aspects of your military existence. Toothpaste tubes had to be tapped square. Everything in your wardrobe had to be perfectly presented and perfectly placed. Shirts had to be folded exactly with the use of a piece of cardboard, then placed in a particular spot; hats had their own space; boots went in three inches from the wall – no closer, no farther – and they could only be put there after you'd spent any free time at night cleaning and polishing them to a mirror-finish, which you would achieve by melting candle wax in a spoon, rubbing it into the boot and polishing in small circles, often for hours. At those times I'd experience a boredom so mind-numbing that it was almost like a spiritual experience.

Everything was done with a view to inspection. The corporal would come in wearing white gloves. You would be standing by your beds (blankets boxed and precisely measured with a stick). He would put his white-gloved hand behind a radiator and if when he took his hand away there was even the slightest speck of dust on his glove he would scream: "You fucking pigs!" I'd find it hard not to laugh. One time he went in to the room next to ours and after a few seconds I heard him shouting: "You fucking pigs! You fucking animals!" Then I heard the window being opened violently and the words: "If you want to be fucking pigs, then be fucking pigs." With that, various items of clothing began being thrown out of the window while his voice became increasingly hysterical. He threw the entire contents of their wardrobes onto the grass below, all the time screaming: "You fucking pigs! Pigs! Pigs! Pigs! Pigs! What are you? Pigs!" For the whole weekend the four occupants of that room had to live in a tent outside the block because, being pigs, they weren't fit to live in the same block as us. Every time I used to look out the window at them I used to crack up with laughter. I used to go to breakfast in the morning and they would come crawling out of the tent, looking very unhappy. Even during drill the four pigs would be singled out for humiliation. The instructor would say to one: "What are you?"

He would reply: "Pig, sergeant."

"WHAT ARE YOU?"

"I'M A PIG, SERGEANT."

Sometimes, even within their earshot, I couldn't stop myself laughing, which used to get me into a lot of trouble. The instructor would shout: "O'Mahoney! What's so fucking funny?" I would go to talk and he would scream: "SHUUUTTT UP!!" As you marched – another thing I loathed – the instructor would measure your strides with his drill stick – a brass-capped cane – and if your steps were longer than was ordained in the regulations he would whack you over the head with the cane.

Unsafe handling of weapons would always be dealt with viciously, although sometimes the instructors would set you up for a beating. One day they lined us up in the corridor. A corporal shouted at me to enter a particular room. I marched in to find an instructor sitting at a desk. I stood to attention and gave him my name, rank and number. He looked me up and down, then said: "Stand at ease." He appeared to return to what he had been doing. After a few seconds he said quietly: "Do us a favour. Pass that weapon to me." On the floor was a sub-machine-gun which looked as if it was in the middle of being cleaned. I bent to pick it up and, bang, I felt a punch in the back of my head. "What the fucking hell do you think you're doing?" he screamed. I remembered too late that the proper procedure when picking up a weapon was to put your foot on it, check to see if it was loaded and generally make sure it was safe before giving it to anyone. I must have been put off guard by the fact that he had spoken to me in a normal tone of voice, which he swiftly abandoned: "YOU FUCKING PIG! YOU FUCKING KILLED ME!" When I recovered from being punched around the room he pointed to Nobby and told me it was mine for a week. Nobby was an old dud shell with a woolly hat on. Anyone who made a mistake when handling a weapon had to carry Nobby around for a week. You had to take it everywhere – to the canteen, on runs, even to bed. They would check to make sure you were carrying it at all times. Nobby was often my companion. The other variation on this theme was the luminous orange hard-hat, which you had to wear at all times for a week if you failed to salute an officer when you passed him. At dinner time the canteen would be dotted with luminous orange hard-hats.

The more efficient we became, the harder they treated us, pushing our minds and bodies to their limits – and beyond. Most recruits, especially those from normal loving backgrounds, could not overcome the shock of army life. They would crack under the bombardment of abuse. At night, people would be talking about running away – or even suicide. Around two-thirds of the recruits in my intake did not finish the course. It seemed to me that the whole selection process was designed to weed out normal people: only the disturbed survived.

7

A Mislaid Testicle

THE SHOCK of constant exercise can do strange things to your body, so I wasn't too worried when after a few weeks' training I noticed a swelling on one of my testicles.

At a routine army medical I showed a doctor, who said he wanted to send me for tests to the Duchess of Kent Military Hospital in Catterick. I was reluctant to go, mainly because I did not want to lose any training days: if you missed too many you faced being "back-squadded" – forced to start your training again with the new intake. Not only did back-squadders have to repeat the awfulness, they were also regarded as losers. The doctor assured me the tests would only take a day, so there was no need to fear being back-squadded. If I'd known what awaited me I would probably have deserted immediately and reported to the nearest prison. It was six months before I emerged from that hospital – minus a testicle.

I remember that period as a blur of pain, boredom and bed sores. What unsettled me most was that throughout that time no-one told me what was wrong. In the army you are told things on a need-to-know basis, but no-one felt that Trooper 24516117 O'Mahoney needed to know anything about his condition. After a while I stopped asking. At first I was given lots of tablets and ordered to stay in bed. I was not allowed to walk anywhere, even to the toilet: I had to piss into a paper cup and shit into a shiny pan. After a few weeks a doctor told me they were going to try to drain off the fluid. This would involve a small operation to insert a tube as thick as a ballpoint pen. Under anaesthetic they inserted the tube into the testicle, then secured it with a small pin. Every time I moved I had the agonising feeling of a tube scraping around inside me. They left it there for weeks, supplementing the treatment only with injections – into my arm, mercifully.

I was receiving so many injections that they began to mess up my veins. In the end they attached a little plastic bin to a vein so that the drugs could be whooshed into me without the nurses having to find an unpunctured spot in my pin-cushion arms. After another long while they thought the tube had become blocked with congealed fluid. They said they were going to clean it by moving it to a new position. I thought this would involve another operation under anaesthetic, but the next morning the nurse said she was going to carry out the procedure on the spot without anaesthetic. I asked her if she was sure. She said yes and drew the curtains. She told me to hold on to the bed as the procedure might hurt a little. She took the pin out, which did not hurt too much. She pulled the tube down, which also did not hurt too much. I thought: "This isn't going to be too bad." I felt her doing something with the tube. She said: "I'm just going to re-insert the pin now." She pushed in the pin and I screamed in a way I had never screamed before – or since. It made me ill for days: the memory of pain can be as bad as the pain itself.

At least once a fortnight they did something horrendous to me. One time they injected me with fluid that had me pissing all over the floor; every now and again they would carry out an exploratory operation, cutting open my groin, pulling everything out and having a look at it, before shoving it back in. They never told me the result of these explorations. There was something inhuman about the way they treated patients in that military environment. When the doctors, who all had military rank, did the rounds the nurses would rush around saying: "Lie neatly in your beds." You would have to lie to attention with the covers folded in the regulation way. The ward sister even threatened to report me for insubordination, because she didn't like the way I spoke to her when she did things that caused me pain. At those times I would shout out: "Oh, you bastard!" I suppose the correct form of address should have been: "Oh, please don't do that, Ma'am. Oh that hurts, Ma'am." Once I asked her if she had ever worked for the Gestapo: she certainly had the personality. Some of the nurses were all right, but in general everyone treated us as if we were just numbers, army property to do with as they saw fit, not living creatures. A few of the staff were so cold and primitive that some nights I half feared I'd wake to find leeches attached to my bollock.

I started to think they were just experimenting on me: perhaps I was some sort of guinea pig? There was no other soldier in there suffering from my ailment – whatever it was. Perhaps they had not seen anything like it before and just wanted to play with it for as long as they could? My testicle – a marvel to military medicine. Of course, in hospital, no matter how ill you are, there's always someone worse off than you. Some of the other soldiers were in a bad way, although they all came and went. Several of them had been injured in Northern Ireland – run over by joyriders or smashed on the head with bricks or blown up or shot. I felt relieved that at least I would never have to serve in the land of my fathers.

I began to get severely depressed. I hadn't wanted to tell my family where I was, so apart from an occasional visit from the Catholic chaplain the only person who came to see me was Alan, my Rhodesian friend. During one visit he suddenly started crying. I knew that something catastrophic must have happened for him to break down like that. I asked him what was wrong. He said that "the kaffirs" had taken over Rhodesia and were going to call it Zimbabwe. He was devastated: his family owned a big farm and he was worried that the blacks would seize it. He was also upset that the struggle had ended before he could get back there with his bayonet. The only good news in his life was that he had got on so well in basic training that the army wanted to make him an officer. They felt he had the qualities to make him a leader of men. He ended up being sent to the officer training-school, the Royal Military Academy at Sandhurst.

He came to see me after an exploratory operation during which I'd been given morphine. I was still a little woozy and my grasp on reality had slipped a little. I said I wanted to escape and needed him to help me. He didn't think this was a good idea. I said I was going to go whether he helped me or not. He tried to dissuade me, but in the end he agreed to take me out, albeit only for a drink in a local pub. He got a wheelchair – there were always lots of them lying around for the many broken soldiers who needed them – and phoned a cab. He made me put on a dressing gown over my pyjamas and told the nurses he wanted to wheel me around the grounds for an hour. In the pub he bought me a pint of lager. I drank it greedily and the world around me began to spin. Dribble cascaded over my lips and my head collapsed onto my chest. I could feel myself drifting off into slumberland. A sergeant I knew came up to me: "What the fuck are you doing here, O'Mahoney?" I couldn't answer: I thought I was going to die. Every now and again I would pull my head up and look around me. Alan, his face lined with worry, was saying things to me, but I couldn't hear him. Finally, he wheeled me out and phoned another cab to take me back to the hospital. By the time we arrived I was making a weird groaning noise. Alan left me in reception – gaga with lolling head – to be found by some nurses I liked. They took me back to my ward and put me in a side room, drawing the curtains around the bed. When the ward sister did her rounds I heard her asking: "What's O'Mahoney doing like that?" The nurses said I'd had a really bad night and had only just got off to sleep, so they had left me there. Behind the curtains I was lying covered in dribble and stinking of drink. Thankfully the ward sister did not check on me.

After six months I was desperate to get out. One day as a doctor examined me I said: "Look, I'm not being funny, but I just want you to cut the thing off." He said it was an option. I said I had been there six months and they could not or would not tell me what was wrong with me: "So just do it." He conferred with his colleagues, then returned: "All right, we'll do it." In normal circumstances you might expect a young man to feel reluctant to have one of his testicles cut off, but by that stage I would have been willing to let them cut off anything and everything if it meant getting out of there. The loss of my testicle seemed a price worth paying. A few days later they came and drew a big red arrow on my right leg – to make sure they did not cut off the wrong one. I had the operation and felt relief more than anything. I'd been told that it would not affect my sexual performance or hinder my chances of fathering children. Apparently, nature equips men with two testicles just in case they mislay one of them in a military hospital.

They gave me a week's sick leave and I went home to Codsall. The only benefit of being in a military hospital was that I had managed to use my ill-health to postpone going to court for the outstanding offences of assault, theft, threatening behaviour and possessing an offensive weapon which I'd committed before joining the army. However, during that week's leave the case was finally heard by Seisdon magistrates. I pleaded guilty. My solicitor said I had since joined the army and had spent the last few months in a military hospital. He said I had put my criminal past behind me and was now determined to contribute something to society by serving my country as a soldier. The magistrate commended my civic spirit and gave me a small fine, £105 with £25 costs. I suspected that my being a soldier had helped secure this leniency.

I had been given a letter to show to my doctor in Codsall. I made an appointment to see him. He read the letter and said: "Ah, testicular cancer." I almost fell off the chair: I had had cancer and no-one had bothered to tell me. My GP said it was the most common cancer among young men. I left the surgery in a daze and spent the rest of the day contemplating an early death. I could think of nothing else. I wandered the streets aimlessly all day, trying to come to terms with the GP's words.

That night I bumped into an old school friend who suggested we went for a drink. Although I'd been told to avoid alcohol because of my medication I didn't think a pint would kill me after all I had endured. The landlord was calling last orders when we arrived, so we ordered two pints each. I drank the first in one go, but as I started on the second I began to feel ill. I told my friend I had to go home and asked him to walk with me. About ten yards from the pub I vomited a spew of water mixed with blood. I fell to the floor. My friend saw all the blood, vomited himself and ran off. Once again I had cause to regret my choice of company. A passerby on the way to Damascus saw me and phoned an ambulance. The ambulance men thought I was drunk. During the journey they lectured me about the crisis in the National Health Service and slagged me off for wasting ambulance time. I was too ill to answer back. They kept me in overnight and released me the next day, warning me not to drink any more alcohol.

Towards the end of my leave I went up to Southport, near Liverpool, to visit my brother Jerry. He took me down to his local pub that lunchtime and bought me a lemonade after I'd told him I couldn't drink. After half an hour of watching my brother drinking his Guinness I decided to join him on the black stuff. I had never drunk it before, but remembered the saying, "Guinness is good for you." I reasoned that it couldn't do me any more harm than the Army Medical Corps. I found that the Guinness didn't make me vomit – it just sent me off my head. We ended up in the bar of Southport Football Club, playing pool with two Liverpudlians. For some reason I got into an argument with them over the game of pool. Things simmered for a little while, but then as one of them leant over the table like a professional to take his shot I clasped my cue in both hands and whacked him over the head with it. The other locals regarded this as a hostile act and the place blew up. I remember standing by the door throwing pool balls at people coming towards me. I don't think I hit anyone because I had triple vision at the time. They managed to push us out into the car park and lock the door, which was made up of little square glass panels. I launched a flying two-legged kick at the door and both feet went straight through the glass panels. I found myself wedged there, hanging upside down, until the police arrived to arrest me. My brother had driven off in the car when he saw the police. A mile down the road he crashed into another car at a set of traffic lights and ended up being done for drink driving.

The army sent an officer to represent me at North Sefton Magistrates' Court, where I was charged with criminal damage. I got my solicitor to blame the incident on the aggressive locals who had provoked the fight. He said I'd flung myself at the door only because I'd feared that my brother was trapped inside the pub. Then the lieutenant stood up to say I was a good soldier who had a fine career ahead of me: my behaviour was completely out of character. He said I had been drinking a drink I did not normally drink and this might have affected my judgment. I was given a conditional discharge, but had to pay £10 compensation with £16 costs. I was pleased with the result. In my eyes it underlined that my status as a soldier offered me a degree of protection from the potential harshness of the law. My only worry was that my previous convictions – the ones I had neglected to declare to the army – had been read out in open court in front of the lieutenant. I was worried he might say something about them when he got back to camp, but after everything else that had happened in recent months I didn't lose any sleep over it.

After recovering from my medical treatment I returned to start my basic training again. Nothing much had changed: the instructors had not become noticeably more compassionate in my absence: I was once more a "pig". Moreover, I was now a pig who had been "living it up skiving in hospital." However, I think they respected me for having put myself back into their care when I could easily have got a medical discharge. Not that they spared me anything as a result. If anything I was subjected to more verbal abuse than the other recruits. The instructors knew me well and knew that their ranting did little more than amuse me. So a sort of reasonably friendly rivalry developed. Towards the end of the seven weeks we had to do an exercise called "Escape and Evasion". This involved being dumped on the Yorkshire Moors for three days with only a compass and map. You had to get from A to B without being caught by the instructors whose job was to hunt you down. One instructor's last words to me were: "We're going to fucking get you, O'Mahoney." Apart from evading capture you had to live off the land. I was determined not to be caught. On the third day, as I neared my destination, I felt pleased that I'd apparently succeeded. The finishing point was in a valley. When I got to the top of the hill overlooking it I saw a Land Rover full of instructors at the pick-up point. They had obviously not even bothered to look for me: they had simply driven there to await my inevitable arrival. I sat at the top of the hill for an hour, hoping vainly that they might drive away. But they weren't going anywhere. They knew I could not finish the exercise until I had reached that point. In the end I just got up and started walking down the hill. As soon as they saw me they jumped out and ran towards me, whooping with joy. The four of them grabbed hold of me and pulled off my shirt. In training we had been taught that if CS gas ever got on our skin we were not to try to wash it off with water, as this would cause severe irritation. They dragged me to a stream, took out a CS gas tablet, and lit it in front of my face so that the gas almost choked me. Then, with CS gas particles covering my naked upper body, they dragged me through the stream. Perhaps they'd just wanted to show they cared.

Towards the end of my basic training the army chaplain stopped me one day to ask my how I was getting on. We had come to know each other quite well during my stay in hospital. I told him I was fine, but was anxious to leave Catterick. He said he would see what he could do. The following day I was called in to the Squadron Office and told that, if I wished, I could go on an HGV driving course instead of hanging around longer to do my tank training. I would then be a lorry driver rather than a tank gunner. The officer said I'd be posted to Germany straight after the two-week course. I reasoned that in civilian life an HGV licence would be of more use to me than the ability to fire the gun of a Chieftain tank, so I agreed. Within three weeks I was sitting on a plane bound for my regiment in Germany. But before I left we had the passing-out parade. I was surprised at how proud I felt that day. I had not wanted to join the army and in many ways I loathed it, yet I felt I had achieved something by completing the course. So many people had laughed when I'd said I was joining the army: they all thought I wouldn't last a week because of the discipline. I had not realised until that day how strong had been my desire to prove them wrong. The need to save face had helped me through. I could not contemplate the shame of going home having failed. I suppose I also felt a sense of achievement because my medical problems meant I'd had to endure more than the other recruits. We marched out onto the parade ground where three rows of proud parents sat watching. I had invited my mother, but she'd told me she wouldn't be able to attend, so I was surprised and pleased to see her standing there with my brothers Michael and Jerry. I found myself filling with emotion. Strange, but true.

8

Give Peace a Chance

LIFE IN Germany at Imphal Barracks in Osnabrück seemed carefree and enjoyable after my recent experiences. There was very little of the clockwork-soldier routine I loathed – the marching, the parades, the spit and polish. This was partly because we spent our days covered in oil and grime from our vehicles. Keeping your vehicle operational was regarded as far more important than having shiny boots. There was also a less rigidly enforced sense of hierarchy, because my immediate superior officer no more wanted to be in the army than I did. Over time I found out that he came from a wealthy and well-connected family. His father had made plain to him that he had to do a stint in "the cavalry" – or else be cut off financially. I discovered that the upper classes called tank regiments "the cavalry" – a reference to their historical origins. There are, of course, differences between horses and tanks, but I suppose that both enable an officer to ride into battle, rather than march vulgarly on foot. Once this particular officer had completed his stint he could look forward to a life cushioned by his father's money. Perhaps it was his daydreaming about this future that gave him an air of vague detachment from the military world: he was certainly a rather hopeless soldier, which made me like him even more. We nicknamed him "Major Disaster", even though major was not his rank. He had a good sense of humour, which in itself distinguished him from the other officers, and he would talk to us like we were friends. He seemed to want acceptance as an equal rather than deference as a superior, which was fine by me: I'd never liked calling officers "Sir" and I refused outright to call corporals "corporal". Some of us came to an agreement with Major Disaster that if we were on our own we'd call him by his first name, saving the use of "Sir" for when more senior officers or "proper soldiers" were nearby.

Social life in Germany mirrored the social life I'd led prior to enlistment – a cocktail of drinking and fighting. The main difference was that I now had a wage from the state to fund my socialising. I found a group of people I liked. Most were from cities, like Liverpool or Belfast, and we shared the same approach to life. Drinking was the main recreation – a hobby shared by almost everyone else in the regiment, which contained its share of full-blown alcoholics. I soon realised people could easily survive in the army as chronic alcoholics, so long as they didn't turn up late for morning parade. The only German word most soldiers learnt was "Bier". The squaddies' world revolved around beer. Sundays, especially, were heavy-drinking days. We would get up around 11 a.m., eat breakfast in the cookhouse, then spend the rest of the day in the Squadron Bar, which was only four doors down from our room. Each squadron had its own bar and each bar gave squaddies credit until pay-day at the end of the month.

One Sunday there was a group of us drinking in the Squadron Bar. An argument developed between two soldiers called Kevin and Jock. Both were pretty drunk. Kevin was slagging off the messy state of Jock's bed-space; this enraged Jock who responded with several mouthfuls of very personal abuse before staggering off to bed. At tea-time we decided to take a brief break from our drinking in order to get something to eat in the cookhouse. We sat down at a table, laughing and joking as we ate our food. The subject turned to Jock. Kevin suddenly got up and said he was going to bed. He lurched off drunkenly and we assumed he had just decided it was time to sleep off the booze. But about ten minutes later the cookhouse door flew open: Kevin stood there stripped to the waist with blood spattered over his hands, chest and face. He said calmly: "Somebody better come. I think I've hurt Jock." We all rushed to the block, leaving Kevin standing there. When we entered the room we found Jock hanging half in and half out of his bed. I could see two deep wounds on his head, one near his cheek, the other on his forehead. There was not much blood, but the blood that was there was deep red, almost black. He was alive, but unconscious and badly hurt. We put him in the recovery position and called out his name, but he didn't respond. On the floor near his head was a large adjustable spanner, smeared with blood. It looked as if Kevin had attacked him as he slept. The ambulance arrived and took Jock away. I never saw him again. Kevin was arrested and installed in the guardhouse. I saw him occasionally being marched at great speed to collect his meals from the cookhouse, but after a week or so he too disappeared, never to be seen again. Questions to sergeants or officers about either man were always met with the same answer: "Surplus to requirements. Forget him." I never did find out what happened to them.

Drinking outside the camp also inevitably led to fighting. Although we had many fights with German civilians and American servicemen, our most bitter battles were fought against British soldiers from rival regiments, especially infantry ones. They had two main reasons for resenting us. First, they knew we regarded them as "grunts" – a lower form of life grunting around the countryside with backpacks while the tracks of our regiment's tanks showered them with mud. Second, they didn't like Irish regiments because we didn't have to serve in Northern Ireland. They thought we were either war-dodging cowards or IRA sympathisers who had joined to get military experience to use against them.

Of course, there were still lots of petty rules that I was always running up against. The army thrived on total bullshit: it was smeared on everything you came into contact with. One rule was that you were not allowed outside the camp without a collar. So if you were caught wearing a t-shirt you were confined to camp for a period. I was always being confined to camp, although my punishment never made much difference to my movements. If I wanted to go out I just climbed over the fence, rather than sign out at the main gate. However, this behaviour once led to my arrest on suspicion of murder.

I had been confined to camp for a week for an offence so trivial that I've forgotten what it was. One night I decided to jump over the fence to go into town. While there I got involved in a mass brawl at a concert by German punks and my shirt got stained with someone's blood. On the same night in another part of town a German woman had been beaten to death with a spanner. The last person she had been seen talking to was believed to have been a British soldier. After a search the next day my blood-stained shirt was found in the wash-basket. When I was first questioned by the German police in the presence of British Military Police I didn't know that someone had been murdered. All that was on my mind was the desire to avoid punishment for having jumped over the fence. So when they asked me about my movements the night before I said I'd been watching television in the camp. They soon established I was lying – and told me about the murder. I felt I had landed myself in one of those nightmarish thrillers in which an innocent man finds himself the prime suspect – and everything he does to show his innocence merely enhances his captors' belief in his guilt. I was held for two days before suddenly being released: a soldier from another regiment had confessed to the murder. He was later given a life sentence. As punishment for jumping the fence I was confined to barracks for another week.

The experience did at least reassure me that the army didn't care about my criminal past. Given that I was held for two days as a murder suspect I felt sure that, as a matter of routine, a check would have been made to see whether I had previous form. I was sure this information would have been passed to the Military Police. Yet no-one said anything. I had been a little worried about my past catching up on me since my appearance in court the previous year over the incident at Southport Football Club. But the officer who had heard my previous convictions being read out had obviously not done anything about them; or, if he had, the army had ignored his information. All these details taken together made me feel confident that my undisclosed criminal past was not something the army cared about – or would ever now act upon.

My two best friends were Paul and Lofty. Both of them hated the army. Paul wanted to be an actor or comedian. He used to stand on the table in the Squadron Bar singing Beach Boys songs, telling jokes and mimicking people. He would often walk around the camp with his beret back to front or pulled down over his ears, marching crab-like, right arm and right leg together, left arm and left leg together. The proper soldiers used to loathe him. Lofty was an even more unlikely recruit. He was extremely laid back, smoking dope and strumming a guitar in his room, the walls of which were covered in Campaign for Nuclear Disarmament and anti-war posters, including the one which said: "Join the army, get a trade, travel to exotic locations, meet interesting people – and kill them." He worked as a clerk in the HQ offices, because he didn't like guns. The real soldiers may have loathed Paul, but they hated Lofty. It must have been one of them who reported his dope-smoking to the Military Police, who raided his room one day looking for evidence. Fortunately, Lofty had smoked everything the night before and got rid of the evidence. The police had to be content with confiscating some of his revolutionary posters, including one featuring the Cuban guerrilla leader, Che Guevara, and another advertising the Paul McCartney record, "Give Ireland Back to the Irish". No-one knew what to make of him. When you asked him why he had joined the army he would say: "It's something I ask myself every day." Like a lot of squaddies he was probably escaping from something worse. He had a days-to-do chart on the inside of his wardrobe door which he ticked off every day. He was one soldier who never got into fights and even went out of his way to get on with the Germans, which really marked him out as a freak. If we were with him we would often get into places from which soldiers were normally barred.

So 1980 drifted past quite pleasantly. I was arrested by the police a few more times over minor incidents, but was never charged: I stole a bike once when I was drunk and didn't have enough money to get a taxi back to barracks; I also stole a taxi-driver's wallet from the jacket he foolishly left on the back seat. The money in it paid for the evening's drinking – but I tipped him well when I got out of the car. In December Paul, a Liverpudlian, ran into my room one morning to tell me that the ex-Beatle John Lennon had been murdered in America. The murder outraged a lot of people in the regiment – many of them were from Liverpool – and that night a huge gang of us went down to an American bar in the town seeking revenge. We beat up every American we could find. I can't remember if any of us were singing the Lennon classic "Give Peace a Chance" at the time.

In February I returned to Codsall for a few days' leave. I learned that my one-time gang had been having trouble with bouncers at the local disco. I decided the bouncers needed to be taught a lesson. I hatched a plan: one of us would go up to the disco on his own; the bouncers would inevitably refuse to let him in; he would then offer to fight the bouncers, who would take the bait and chase him into the car park – where about 15 of us would be waiting behind a fence armed with knives, spanners, metal bars and whatever other implements we could find. Everything went to plan. As soon as the bouncers chased our friend into the car park we laid into them. There was a brief vicious struggle before they ran back to the safety of the disco and slammed the doors shut. However, in their haste to escape they left behind one of their mates. I and another slammed into him with lumps of wood. He was screaming desperately: "Let me in! Let me in!" Eventually they opened the door and let him in, fighting us back from the entrance. They managed again to slam shut the studded doors. We went around to the side where there were huge earthen plant pots. We picked these up and started hurling them through the disco's windows. The sounds of breaking glass and women screaming mingled with the disco beat. When we ran out of earthen pots we threw in everything else we had – bricks, bottles, bits of wood. The disco was full – probably about 500 people – and we could hear the DJ making an urgent appeal to the crowd: "Help the doormen! Help the doormen!" Suddenly the doors burst open and a swarm of angry people flew out after us. We were heavily outnumbered – there must have been about 100 of them – but we stood and fought. Some of them had armed themselves with plates from the kitchen which they threw at us. The fight spilled from the car park onto the nearby estate. When the police finally arrived we were fighting in people's gardens. There were bodies everywhere, lying among the debris of glass and plates. Not surprisingly, the police knew who to arrest and, naturally, I was among them. I spent the night in custody before being released. The police told me the court case would not be for a few months. By this stage I wasn't too worried about notching up yet another conviction for violence. I hardly thought it would jeopardise my army career. Indeed, I'd found that contempt for civilians was one of the hallmarks of army life, so I felt confident that a conviction for bashing a few despised civvies wouldn't count against me. And, anyway, I knew by now that my status as a soldier would ensure lenient treatment from the magistrates.

I flew back to Germany and into a barracks whispering with rumours. The main rumour was that the Ministry of Defence was considering abandoning the policy of not sending Irish regiments to Northern Ireland. The question was: which of us war-dodgers would be the first to go? Everyone thought they would send the Irish Guards because they were foot-soldiers armed with the standard Self-Loading Rifle (SLR). Most of us had not even seen an SLR, let alone fired one. As members of a tank regiment we used sub-machine-guns. But we should have had enough experience of military logic by then to know that the army would not do what was rational and sensible. Within a fortnight the news landed like a mortar among us: the 5th Royal Inniskilling Dragoon Guards were going to be given the privilege of being the first Irish regiment to be sent to the six counties. Our four and a half month tour of duty would start on 10 April 1981. What was more, we'd be going to the historical recruitment base of our regiment – Enniskillen in County Fermanagh. Depression followed the panic which followed the shock. I realised that for many the derogatory nickname "war-dodgers" had been neither unkind nor inaccurate. It became apparent that a lot of people had genuinely joined the regiment in the belief they would never have to serve in Northern Ireland. The only ones who seemed enthusiastic were a handful of Fermanagh Protestants. The regiment still attracted a lot of people from the Enniskillen area, all Protestants. Some of them had left the area because the safety of their families had been compromised through links with the Crown. A lot of them had relations in the Royal Ulster Constabulary (RUC) or the Ulster Defence Regiment (UDR). The idea of returning to patrol their own streets appealed greatly to the staunch loyalists: some of them made it plain they had scores to settle with the Catholic population. I imagined how I might behave if sent back to patrol Codsall with a rifle.

I felt strangely neutral about the prospective tour. I had been in the army for two years by then and Germany had begun to bore me. I was not raring to go, but half of me felt quite excited by the idea. Then just as the regiment absorbed the fact that they were going, another piece of news caused further anxiety. The IRA prisoner Bobby Sands started a hunger strike on 1 March; other IRA and Irish National Liberation Army (INLA) prisoners were ready to join the hunger strike. The television news bulletins became the most popular programmes, and suddenly everyone seemed to be discussing the politics of Northern Ireland, with special reference to the hunger strike. The most common feeling among the lower ranks was that Mrs Thatcher should have given the IRA prisoners what they wanted, namely, status as political prisoners, rather than have them treated as ordinary criminals. Our reasoning was that under the Geneva Convention those Provos already in custody would then be prisoners of war with no release date, no trials and no appeals; and, most importantly, we'd then be allowed to execute summarily any of their comrades we subsequently caught not wearing uniform "on active service".

Each night on the news we would watch tensions rising in Northern Ireland. Soldiers started getting more army barmy – the barracks suddenly seemed full of fitness fanatics. I had to go back into hospital for a few weeks and so missed the week of special training at the Sennelager base – known as Tin City – where soldiers were sent to sharpen up their urban warfare skills prior to going to Ireland. I heard the week had been a fiasco: their trainers had not been impressed with their military skills. But what could they expect? We were a tank regiment; we weren't trained as foot-soldiers.

When I got back to base in late March I was told to report to a major's office in the main administrative block. The major said he knew my parents were Irish Catholics and that I had relations living near the border. He said if I strongly objected to going to Northern Ireland I would not have to go. I said I wanted to go, although I didn't explain why. My desire had nothing to do with going to fight for Queen and country. It was far more basic and simple than that: I just wanted to be with my friends. My loyalty was to them – and I had no intention of being the one waving at the gate as they left. To me it was like they were going out for a fight in the car park and I was going to join them.

The week before we went everyone was drinking heavily. One night a group of us got a taxi back to the barracks. We were all drunk. With us was one of the Ulster Protestants who was keen to get over to Ireland. For some reason he decided to jump out of the taxi before it had stopped moving. He fell badly and ended up smashing his back and losing a kidney. Somehow it seemed like a bad omen. On our last night in Germany the barracks had the atmosphere of a funeral parlour. Gloom, gloom and more gloom. Anyone who had a girlfriend was phoning home to say goodbye to her. It was like watching a bad film. Then when I thought things could not get gloomier the news came through that the IRA hunger striker Bobby Sands had just been elected to parliament for the constituency of Fermanagh-South Tyrone – the area where we would be based. There were about ten of us watching TV in the Squadron Bar when we heard. The news did not go down well: it could mean only one thing – we were going to be stuck for four and a half months in an area crawling with Provos and their sympathisers. I tried to lighten the deathly atmosphere with a joke. I said that if the locals mistreated us we'd at least know who our MP was to complain to.

Everyone turned to look at me, but no-one laughed.

9

Muppet in Hollywood

INSIDE THE Hercules aircraft that would take us to Northern Ireland we sat dejectedly. No-one spoke.

The stale air seemed heavy with foreboding. Outside, the ground crew shouted and laughed as they readied the plane for take-off. To them it was just another day; to us it seemed like our last. We sat facing each other on hard wooden benches that stretched down each side of the cavernous interior. There were no windows, just a large hole at the back of the aircraft through which everyone and everything came and went. The last pieces of kit were wheeled up the ramp. Then we all watched as the plane's huge back door lifted off the ground and moved slowly upwards, gradually blacking out the natural light before slamming shut like the lid of a coffin.

Like everyone else, I had my full backpack of kit in front of me. Unlike everyone else, I did not have the standard infantryman's Self-Loading Rifle. I would not be allowed one of those until I had done my week's training at the Hollywood base on the outskirts of Belfast.

The engines started up with a blast of noise that jolted us into a more alert state of anxiety. The plane began to move. The sound of the engines got more frantic and the back door started vibrating wildly. Someone pointed at it and shouted above the noise: "It's falling apart." Everyone laughed, but uncomfortably: we all started looking intently at the door thinking he might be right. But with a final scream of effort the plane took off. During the flight a few people tried cracking jokes, but nothing could dispel the heavy feeling of gloom.

We touched down at Aldergrove Airport near Belfast. As the back door wound its way to the ground my mind filled with images of grinning Provos lifting their sniper's rifles to their shoulders.

"OK, move!" shouted the senior officer.

We got up from the benches, slung our packs on our backs and began filing out into a massive hangar. Everyone looked lost. Around 50 yards away was another group of soldiers whose mood contrasted sharply with ours. They were overflowing with jubilation, laughing and playing like children at break-time. I soon discovered the reason for their happiness: they were on their way back to Germany. I don't know whether it was deliberate army policy always to have soldiers from incoming regiments filing past those from outgoing ones. Perhaps they thought the sight of soldiers on their way home in one piece would give us something to look forward to. If so, they were wrong: seeing the delight of the outgoing soldiers only intensified our misery.

Soon the barking started. An officer with a clipboard began shouting out names, squadrons and destinations within County Fermanagh. We had been told in Germany we were going to be split up and sent to bases at Belcoo, Lisnaskea, Belleek, Rosslea, Newtownbutler and St Angelo. So I already knew I was going to be separated from Lofty and Paul, but the reality still came as a blow. I trusted them: I knew they would have looked out for me, and I for them; in times of danger we would have been there for one another. But it was not to be. I was going to Lisnaskea; they were going to Belleek. I felt terrible, especially when I saw they'd been put with several of the regiment's most gormless prats. I felt especially sorry for Lofty, who was one of those who had joined the regiment believing he would never get posted to Northern Ireland. He had always said he would never shoot anyone, whatever happened. He hated unnecessary violence. In Germany when fighting broke out around him, which sometimes happened when he went out with me, he would look pained, put his head in his hands and say mournfully: "Oh, no!" His pacifist tendencies were well known and he could have been kept behind in Germany to work in the offices, but they seemed to make a point of sending him.

Once the division had taken place we stood bewilderedly in our groups. I nodded at Paul, who smiled back weakly. Lofty was just staring at the ground: he seemed to be muttering to himself. Nearby were several seemingly civilian lorries: some had the markings of removal firms, others advertised well-known brands of frozen food.

The officer with the clipboard pointed to the lorries and said: "Your transport to Bandit Country, gentlemen."

I had not given much thought to how we were going to get to Fermanagh, but I had assumed the army would at least put us in vehicles with some sort of armour-plating. The thought of travelling through terrorist heartlands in unprotected lorries managed to lower morale even further. However, we were not given too much time to dwell on what awaited. The barking started again and the first group were led to their lorry. Paul and Lofty's group went before mine – they got one of the removal lorries. I walked over quickly to say goodbye to them. They were sitting on the floor looking as unhappy as I had ever seen them.

"Keep your head down, cunt," said Paul.

I smiled and said I was sure they'd get him before they got me. We bantered for a few more seconds until I saw my group move off. I said: "See you later you fucking scouse bastard." I felt awful leaving them, just gutted. A sergeant had directed my group towards a refrigerated meat lorry. Bad omen, I thought: frozen meat.

The sergeant said: "Sit in the back and don't say a fucking word. Don't make a noise until these doors open again. Even if the lorry stops – you might just be at traffic lights."

We got in and sat on the floor. The sergeant gave an evil smile before slamming shut the heavy back door and throwing us into total darkness. I had never felt so trapped and helpless. I heard the latch being locked and realised that if we were attacked we wouldn't be able to make our own way out.

The lorry started up and moved off. I could not see the other soldiers but I could smell their fear – and I am sure they could smell mine. I imagined machine-gun bullets tearing through the lorry's flimsy skin; I wondered what would be left to put in a coffin if a rocket-propelled grenade hit us. The journey in that black box lasted around three hours, although every second seemed to last an hour. I had heard stories about the IRA setting up their own checkpoints in the border area, so my heart started racing whenever the lorry stopped. You could sense the relief when it moved off again.

When not listening out for the Provo traffic police I thought morbidly of what might be in store in the months ahead. In the silence of the darkness I thought of Paul, Lofty and my family. Would I see them again? And, with Paul and Lofty, if we survived would we all be in the same state? After all, you didn't necessarily die if you were hit: you might just be wounded hideously. Which one of us would get hit? Would it be me? I imagined a reunion with Paul and Lofty; I could see myself being pushed towards them in a wheelchair; I could see them having to shake the stump where my hand had been. Everyone felt that at least one person in the regiment was going to get it. As my eyes got used to the darkness I could make out faces in the lorry. I looked into those faces and all I could think was: which one? Who is going to get taken out? I just hoped it wasn't me or my friends. Finally, the lorry stopped and I could hear English accents outside. Someone pulled open the door and the light greeted us.

Lisnaskea was a small camp built close to a school, which I assumed was meant to deter the Provos from launching mortar attacks. There were about ten Portakabins and three brick buildings surrounded by barbed wire. The conditions in the camp were squalid. I found myself sleeping in a gym where the beds were three-high and a foot apart. Even the regimental magazine – not known for subversive criticism – said it was a scene of human-rights violations. But that night the cramped squalor did not worry us too much: the psychological torture of the journey down had left us exhausted and we were grateful for any bed.

The next day I put on civilian clothes and got in an unmarked car to be taken to Hollywood Barracks near Belfast for a week's anti-terrorist training. Once again the mode of transport did not fill me with a sense of security, but I could at least look out the windows and, if necessary, open the car door. The handgun in the glove compartment made me feel a little better too. The early part of the journey, travelling along isolated country roads, filled me with apprehension, but the last stretch on the motorway made me more relaxed. I hardly took in any of the scenery: I was too busy looking out for snipers and men in balaclavas manning checkpoints.

At Hollywood I found myself in a group of about 20 soldiers from different regiments. We sat in a room with a large television at the front.

A major walked in, marched to the front and said: "If you're going to die, we might as well tell you why." He then played a video which condensed Ireland's history into 30 minutes. When the video finished he began talking to us in a matter-of-fact tone, as if he were merely stating the obvious. He opened his talk by saying that the film had probably left us more confused than enlightened, but that this did not really matter. The essential fact, he said, was that as British soldiers we were little more than piggies-in-the-middle in a baffling tribal conflict, the intricacies of which need not concern us too greatly. All we really needed to bear in mind as we went about our duties were the simple equations: Catholic = IRA = Bad and Protestant = British = Good.

He said he did not mean to give offence to any Catholics in the group, if there were any, as British Catholics were obviously different from Irish Catholics. He said he knew also he was being deeply unfair to the many Irish Catholics who did not support the IRA. However, his purpose was merely to identify the tribal grouping from which the threat to our lives was most likely to come. And the simple fact of the matter was that we didn't need to be as wary of Protestants. He rounded off his talk by saying that of course Britain should give Northern Ireland back to the Irish, but the province was such a good training ground that the army didn't want to let it go. He said that in most years more soldiers were killed on exercises in Germany than died at the hands of terrorists in Northern Ireland. Everyone was so taken aback by his cynical frankness that after he left no-one really said anything. The only comment was from a Liverpudlian who asked: "Was he taking the piss?"

The major's last observation about the statistical improbability of our coming to any harm had not been absorbed by the course instructors who for the whole of that week told us we were definitely going to die. No doubt about it. Every second sentence that emerged at high pitch from their spit-flecked mouths assured us that our incompetence as soldiers meant the Provos would certainly kill us.

The scene of most of our training was what looked like the set of *Coronation Street*: several rows of the exteriors of two-up-two-down terraced houses. Videos filmed us patrolling these streets and captured on tape our pitiful attempts to negotiate the various hazards put in our path. Cardboard cut-outs of various "friendly" and "non-friendly" people appeared suddenly at windows – usually to be blasted indiscriminately by me and my fellow "Professionals". I lost count of the number of vicars and women and children we collectively managed to massacre as we wandered the streets hopelessly in our numbered fluorescent jackets. Occasionally a balaclava-clad Provo cut-out would appear: he tended to escape with his cardboard life.

An instructor told us that at some stage in Northern Ireland we would all have a sniper's rifle trained on our heads. Sometimes as we patrolled the streets they would set off an explosive charge in a house. When we ran for cover behind a car they would detonate something in the car. Ranting and raving in the way that only army NCOs know how, they would point out that we were supposed to check everything we used for shelter. They often gave the impression of being in despair.

One of them kept shouting: "You're going to die. Paddy will look for fools like you – off-the-ball, day-dreaming, dead."

After each exercise we would watch our mistakes on video. Once as we carried out a house search I walked into a room to find a package on the floor. Smoke began to billow from it. I picked it up and ran out into the street where I dumped it on the road. I thought I'd done quite well.

The instructor disagreed: "You fucking muppet! You stupid fucking muppet!"

When we gathered in the debriefing room he ordered me to stand on a chair in front of everyone. He said: "I want you to take a long hard look at this man." Everyone stared at me. "Does anyone know why I want you all to look at him?" No-one spoke. "It's because this man is going to get you all killed." The stares became harder. The instructor shouted: "You're a fucking muppet, aren't you O'Mahoney?"

I said I was.

He pointed out that, while I might have saved the lives of the civilians in the house, I had taken a bomb out into a street full of soldiers, whose lives were more valuable.

He said: "What are you?"

I said again: "I'm a muppet."

Then, in case anyone in the room had still not deduced what I was, he screamed in agreement: "Yes, you're a fucking muppet."

We would do our best, but no matter what we did they would make us feel that we'd not just made a mistake, but had committed a truly life-ending error.

"You're going to die! You're going to die!" was the response to almost everything we did. After a few days we all started to believe them. At night I would lie in bed thinking: "God, what am I doing here? I'm doing everything wrong. I *am* going to die."

I received a few rudimentary lessons in the workings of the Self-Loading Rifle, but they hardly served to bolster my morale. A proper infantryman should have been capable of stripping down an SLR blindfolded. I needed natural light and the help of my colleagues. On the firing range I hardly hit the target.

Once an instructor bent down beside me and screamed: "Don't apply for the marksman's course yet, you useless cunt." I thought the only way I would survive in Ulster was if I could drive an armoured personnel carrier – a "Pig", as it was known – in a built-up area. A few months earlier I'd been sent on a course to Hull to learn how to drive one. At least on that course I had felt competent driving around smashing into barricades and ramming wrecked cars. When the Pigs were battened down the driver only had a six-by-three inch perspex window to see out of. We were taught that rioters tried to disable Pigs by throwing paint on that window, so in the water container for the window-wipers we were told to put paint-stripper. However, I didn't get to act on this wisdom: I didn't even see a Pig during my whole time in Northern Ireland, let alone get to drive one.

Then our anti-terrorist training was all over. After a week in which we had apparently not done anything right we were told we were now trained and ready for action. A soldier from my regiment came to take me back to Fermanagh, again in an unmarked car. He had been out on patrol a few times already and was talking like a veteran. If anything, the week's training had made me feel even more vulnerable and I slightly resented my colleague's apparently relaxed state.

As we passed through a town near to where we were going he said: "Oh, I'll show you around here." He drove to a loyalist housing estate where a pipe band was practising their tunes. We parked a few hundred yards away from them. They started marching up the street towards us, led by a few aggressive-looking men competing with each other to see who could hurl batons highest into the air.

My companion said: "This is Ulster."

The band marched past us. Several of the pipers looked at us suspiciously.

I said: "What a bunch of fucking edibles." They came back down past us: their marching seemed more frenzied. I began to feel unsafe and uncomfortable: perhaps they could smell my Irish Catholic blood. I said: "Get me out of here, you cunt."

On the journey back I felt a sort of anger at being surrounded by so much hostility. None of these people knew me, but as far as I could see lots of them already hated me – and wanted to do me harm. "Fuck them," I thought. I wasn't going to let them: it was as simple as that – I wasn't going to let them. There was no way I was going back to Codsall in either a coffin or a wheelchair. I didn't give a toss about the politics of the situation. I just wanted to survive – and was determined to do so in the best way I knew how. I would survive by dealing ruthlessly with any potential threats. And, as far as I was concerned, anybody I did not know personally was a threat.

I would crush those threats before they crushed me.

10

Beer for the Boys

THE SERGEANT called a troop meeting before I went out on my first patrol.

He was probably the most experienced soldier in our regiment. I was told he had joined us from another regiment and had already done a few tours of duty in Northern Ireland. I hadn't had much contact with him before, but I knew from talking to other soldiers that he was highly regarded. He tended to do things by the book but, unlike a few of the other NCOs and officers, he did at least inspire confidence in his military capability.

There must have been about 20 of us gathered in front of him. We had all been in Ireland for a week. Most had already been out on the streets. Some tried to give off the nonchalant air of veterans; others still looked as bewildered and fearful as we all had on first stepping off the plane at Aldergrove.

There were no officers present in the meeting room. The sergeant began by saying that now we had acclimatised ourselves to our new environment he wanted to underline a few points which we ought to bear in mind for the rest of the tour. He picked on a few mistakes that people were making while out on patrol and in dealings with the natives. He reminded us that when on patrol or at vehicle checkpoints we were not under any circumstances to do or say anything that would identify our officers as officers. In the Provos' score chart of hits an officer was always worth more points than an ordinary squaddie. He said officers on the street would not wear badges of rank in order to make more difficult the sniper's task of identifying them. So we had to make sure we did not inadvertently help snipers by, for instance, addressing officers as "Sir", especially in front of potential terrorists (that is, all Irish Catholics). Of course, once back in barracks we had to maintain the correct forms of address.

He mentioned a few other minor points before coming to the matter I felt had probably been at the forefront of his mind. He said that if, for whatever reason, we had to open fire on anyone, and we wounded him, we had to ensure he didn't live: we had to kill him outright. He said that surviving victims might be able to dispute the army's version of events – and the last thing any of us needed was a prolonged investigation and a messy court case in which we had to go back and forward to Ireland to be examined by "cunts in wigs".

In case we had not grasped what he was saying he

summarised things in words I have never forgotten: "Just shoot the fucker dead and we'll make it up from there." No-one raised any objections, but I could see a few people looking uncomfortable. I wasn't one of them: I thought the sergeant's advice extremely astute and I intended following it in the event of a firefight with suspected terrorists. Perhaps to lighten the atmosphere he finished by saying there would be a crate of beer for the first one of us to kill a paddy.

There are many events during that tour that I can remember with astonishing clarity. Even today I can replay each second in my mind, because I lived so intensely at the time. One of these is my first patrol. We stood at the gates of the Lisnaskea camp in two "bricks" – squads of four – cradling our SLRs in our arms. One of the things that the instructors at Hollywood banged into us was that soldiers on patrol were at their most vulnerable passing through the camp gates. Terrorists do not know which routes you will take when you are on the streets, because you always vary them. All they know for sure is that you must pass through the camp gates at the beginning and end of your patrol. I stood there as alert as I had ever been in my life. I imagined what awaited on the other side. I thought of the gates opening and of us moving out into a hail of bullets. Or perhaps there would be just one sniper who would fire just one bullet which would hit me straight in the head.

Our sergeant gave a signal to the two soldiers at the reinforced gates. They swung them open suddenly at great speed. "OK, go!" shouted our sergeant. We sped out through the gates and into the world of danger – or so it seemed. The instructors at Hollywood had done such a thorough job in alerting us to potential hazards that nothing and no-one seemed innocent. Each brick took a different side of the road.

A car came towards us. Why was it going so fast? I pushed the butt of my SLR more tightly into my shoulder, ready to swing the muzzle round and blast the Provo bastard. The car passed us, a middle-aged woman with glasses in the driver's seat.

We walked on at high speed, moving in zig-zags, looking at everything with intensity. I tried to remember everything I had been taught: "Make yourself a difficult target. Move from side to side. Don't lean against walls." We would stop occasionally and stoop down. Everything looked so normal – and that unnerved me. Further down the street a car pulled away as we approached. He had moved off a bit too fast for my liking. I felt my finger tightening on the trigger, but he too drove past without incident.

The streets seemed quiet, the houses unoccupied. Then suddenly a door opened and a child ran screaming out. My heart seemed to expand with the shock. The child ran past, playing aeroplanes: he didn't seem to register our presence. An old man stood at his fence giving us a look of pure hatred. In another street a young mother picked up her child and moved quickly indoors. I wondered why she had done that: did she know something? We had been told that sometimes the Provos warned people about imminent attacks on army patrols, so if a street seemed unusually quiet we had to be especially alert. The problem was that almost every street seemed unusually quiet. Everything held out the possibility of impending danger, so I couldn't relax for a second. Every step was a step taken in a state of high anxiety. By the time we got back to camp two hours later I felt exhausted, not physically – we had probably only covered a few miles – but mentally. I slumped on my bed, totally shattered. The thought of having more than four months of this still to do filled me with dread.

Over the next few days I had my introduction to what was to be our other main pastime – manning vehicle checkpoints, the dreaded VCPs. There were two types – mobile and permanent. We would set up the mobile ones while out on patrol. Usually, a helicopter would drop us in the countryside and our officer would choose a spot on an isolated road where we would start stopping cars. We would stay there for half an hour or so and then tramp across fields to another spot to do the same.

If you were not checking cars you had to take up firing positions on the ground which, being Irish ground, was usually soaking wet. However, I still preferred the mobile VCPs to the permanent ones, which tended to guarantee you several days of the most astonishing boredom. The permanent VCPs were fortified: they had a machine-gun position at either end in a "sangar", of which there were two types. One was the size of two telephone boxes, made of breeze-blocks and sandbags. In these you had to stand to look out of the three viewing holes. The other was even smaller, made only of sandbags. You had to crawl into it and lie down for 12 hours gazing down the barrel of a heavy machine-gun which pointed through a shoebox-size hole across a deserted country road.

Motorists would drive past the first machine-gun post and zig-zag into the centre where their licences would be checked before they were allowed to zig-zag past the other post. I much preferred to be in the middle zone checking drivers. Squaddies in the machine-gun sangars used to spend their shifts making tea or heating tinned food on the small camp cooker, masturbating and fantasising about opening fire on the occasional passing motorist.

If you wanted a piss or a shit you could ask someone to relieve you while you relieved yourself, but it was hardly worth the trouble. Toilets in the main central area were only holes in the ground. So soldiers in the outer sangars usually used a carrier bag into which they would do their business. They would then tie it up and drop it outside until the end of their "stag" (slang for their work shift), when they would take it to the main area to bury it.

When it rained the sangar flooded and I would find myself squatting in mud: when the sun shone the stench and the occasional rat would keep me awake. And staying awake was difficult when all you did all day was stare down a machine-gun barrel at cows or sheep. An occupational hazard in those conditions was piles caused by sitting for hours in the damp while eating tinned garbage that provoked either constipation or diarrhoea.

In those early days I found people recoiling from me as I stuck my face in drivers' windows. I had had my two front teeth knocked out by a nightclub bouncer's knuckle-duster a few months before arriving in Ireland. I realised that my teeth's absence gave me a slightly intimidating look, at least when combined with a head shorn of hair, a face smeared with camouflage cream and a rifle that even civilians could tell I was holding inexpertly. An officer even said to me one day that I needed to get my teeth sorted out as I looked like a bit of a thug. It was arranged for me to visit the army dentist at Omagh to get fitted with a new plate of false teeth.

My missing teeth did not alter significantly my Midlands accent, which the locals seemed to understand easily enough. Not all English regional accents translated well in Northern Ireland: another soldier from Tyneside kept having problems making himself understood. Questions like, "Where ya gooin', old un?" tended to result in blank looks from the Fermanagh public. Tail-backs would develop at checkpoints as baffled drivers tried to work out what he was saying. At first he thought the Irish were mocking him, but officers realised his accent was the problem and they ordered him to spend his shifts where he would not come into contact with civilians. He ended up spending most of the tour sitting sullenly in a sangar with only a machine-gun and cows for company.

Throughout those first few weeks the tension rose in the camp and on the streets as our local MP, Bobby Sands, slowly starved himself to death. Around 1,000 people took part in what was described in the local paper as "the most impressive ever Easter Sunday commemoration in Fermanagh" when the IRA fired a volley of shots over the grave of a local IRA man, Louis Leonard, at Donagh. The same paper carried a warning from the South Fermanagh Provisional IRA. It read: "Anyone who is to be found informing or collaborating with the security forces – RUC, UDR or British Army – will be dealt with without mercy."

This paragraph gave us an idea. We started giving special treatment to certain republicans, especially those we regarded as sympathisers on the margins of the movement. If we came across one of them in the street we would be overly friendly. For instance, we might pat him gently on the arm and start laughing, as if he had told us something funny. Or else we would let him walk off and then shout after him something like: "Cheers, Sean. Thanks for that." or "Speak to you Wednesday, then." This behaviour seemed to disturb them more than outright harassment. One publican from

Newtownbutler even pleaded with me once to stop doing it because people were beginning to think he was an informer.

"That's the idea, shitface," I said.

I didn't mind harassing republicans on the street, but I hated searching their houses, especially if there were children present. We never found anything – nor did we really expect to find anything. As far as I could see, the primary purpose of searches was to harass the occupants, to put pressure on them and to remind them that we knew what they were up to. We did not kick in doors and charge in: we were more cold and calculating than that.

I remember doing one with the RUC in those first few weeks. We were told it was the home of an IRA man on the run. Initially, I stayed in the front garden while the RUC men entered the run-down council house. After a few minutes I walked in myself. The inside was tidy, but spartan. A woman stood in the front room. Her two boys, aged about eight and ten, stood next to her with their arms around her. I could tell they were protecting her rather than seeking protection. I had clung to my own mother in the same way in the face of my father's brutality. I recognised the look on their faces, that expressionless gaze of silent hatred.

A coal fire blazed behind the woman. On the mantelpiece were framed photos of her family, although none included her absent husband. I assumed she had hidden those in case we seized them. One of the boys looked at me. I smiled instinctively. But he didn't respond: all he could see was my rifle and my British uniform. The woman spoke with a soft quiet voice, which somehow made everything worse. I looked around and noticed Jesus Christ looking down on us all from a large wooden crucifix on the wall. He had that same mournful expression I remembered from the picture in my own family home. I imagined those boys praying to Him for my sudden death, like I had prayed for my father's. I hoped that they too would get a negative response from the Lord. I left the house feeling deflated and uneasy. It was at those times that I felt like a Judas betraying my own kind. The RUC men seemed happy with their day's work, talking about "the lying whore" and her "Fenian murdering bastard" of a husband. We never raided Protestant houses looking for loyalist terrorists. The latter were always mentioned in terms of approval: soldiers and police regarded them as part of the common good.

I lived in the anticipation of being shot or blown up. We had all written our blood group in indelible ink on the underside of our combat-jacket pockets; and in Germany I had been given two metal identity tags containing my name, rank and serial number. You were supposed to tie one tag around your neck and attach the other to one of your bootlaces. The idea was that if you were blown to bits your remains would still be identifiable – or at least one of your feet would be.

In those early weeks there was one incident which could have necessitated the use of my ID tags. One of our regular tasks was to check the area's culverts (large drains which allow water to pass under a road). The IRA had frequently used culverts to hide bombs which they detonated under passing military or police vehicles. To prevent culverts being used in this way the army had placed bars or security gates across them. One day we were told that a milk churn had been spotted under a culvert: our job was to clear the area while the bomb-disposal people went to work. A helicopter dropped us in a field near the culvert. I could not see what there was to clear as we were in the middle of an empty field. However, we spread out several hundred yards away from the suspected bomb and remained there staring at it for about eight hours. During that time an army spotter plane flew over, taking photos of the ground to see if there were any buried command wires leading from the bomb to the terrorists' planned detonation point. Suddenly we got the order to evacuate the area. When we got back to base we were told that the plane had spotted two command wires. One led from the culvert to an overlooking hill; the other started several hundred yards away from the culvert – roughly where we had taken cover – and finished on top of another hill. We had been sitting on a bomb: the Provos had obviously hoped to hit a security forces' vehicle with the culvert bomb, then have a second crack at the soldiers who arrived to pick up the pieces. Both bombs had failed to detonate, but the experience drove home to us how vulnerable we were.

However, boredom, not the Provos, caused our regiment's first casualty. I was not present at the incident, but I heard the commotion on the radio. A soldier on duty in one of the outer sangars of a permanent VCP had probably decided to relieve his boredom by cleaning his General Purpose Machine-Gun (GPMG). There was, after all, little else to do. He started stripping the gun down, but left in a bullet-belt. He must have removed one of the gun's fail-safe components and then accidentally pulled the trigger, because the GPMG suddenly started spraying bullets all over the place. Unfortunately, one of them slammed in to the thigh of a soldier standing further down the road. The gun kept firing despite the gunner's efforts to stop it. Finally, he had to twist the bullet-belt to jam it. We had been taught various code words to use on the radio to cover incidents for which we needed assistance. For instance, you had to shout "Contact! Contact! Contact!" if someone shot at you. However, there was no code for shooting yourself. I could hear the soldiers on the radio asking for help, but not being quite sure what to say.

There had not been any civilians nearby at the time and the wounded soldier was not critically injured, so there was no major inquiry. To me the incident just underlined that we were the wrong soldiers in the wrong place at the wrong time.

11

A Shot in the Foot

I HAD been at Lisnaskea for less than a fortnight when I found myself transferred to Fermanagh's main military base.

I was sent to St Angelo Barracks, sited on a disused airfield outside Enniskillen, to join a new roving unit of 16 soldiers. The idea was that we'd be available to float around the county at short notice to fill in gaps and provide back-up where necessary. When we first arrived a few of the squaddies were terrified because the camp was surrounded by hills. We had been taught that you had to take the high ground in order to launch a successful attack. And we remembered our instructors' promise that at some stage in Northern Ireland all of us would have a rifle trained on our heads. Taken together, these observations convinced a few soldiers that the hills were swarming with snipers. For the first few days I noticed one squaddie stooping his head whenever he came out of a building. He stopped doing it after I ridiculed him by asking if he'd lost some money.

The conditions were a huge improvement on Lisnaskea: there were even women walking around – Ulster Defence Regiment Greenfinches who worked in the operations room. The base comprised about 20 Portakabins on an old runway and acted as the nerve centre for all operations in the county. Each Portakabin was surrounded by six-foot high grey breeze-block blast-walls, which were meant to give protection from mortars. Several of the Portakabins acted as cramped sleeping quarters for our soldiers and others were used by the Ulster Defence Regiment (UDR) for various things. One was used by a squad of eight SAS men and soldiers from our regiment's Close Observation Team, who were specially trained in undercover surveillance. Others contained the radio room, the intelligence cell (which collated information about republican activity), the stores, the TV room and the REMF. I never found out what the letters REMF stood for. To us they signified a room full of uniform-wearing clerks who only blacked up and carried rifles to pose for photographs for the regimental magazine. The unofficial transcription of the words REMF was: Rear Echelon Mother Fuckers. The camp, like the others I visited, also had its own shop. These shops were always run by Asians and were known as "Chogi" shops. They were not walk-in-and-browse concerns: they were more like school tuck shops with a raised counter and serving hatch. You queued up, peered in, found they had run out of the sweets you wanted, then left. There was also a small shooting range and a helicopter pad, used by Wessex and Lynx helicopters.

I was pleased to see there was a bar and a proper canteen, which seated about 50. At first I thought I might finally get to eat some decent food, but I soon discovered that the cooks served only the most diabolical slop: allegedly-corned-beef hash, allegedly-chicken curry (bones included) and a stew which seemed to contain the unidentifiable flesh of long-buried animals dug up and reheated. We ate off stainless-steel trays indented with three spaces, presumably to help maintain discipline on the plate. "Diggers" (army slang for knives, forks and spoons) were provided, but most squaddies preferred to use their own snap-together camping utensils as the diggers looked as if they were cleaned irregularly. Tea, known as "slurp", was always available and was drunk from half-pint black-plastic field mugs.

I found myself sharing living space mainly with soldiers I only knew vaguely – and, in most cases, wished I didn't know at all. Several of them were staunch Ulster loyalists whose hatred of Catholics made them regard me as suspect. The more I got to know them the more I thought that sending them home to police their own community was not one of the British Empire's most inspired deeds. One of them I nicknamed Nasty: he was a loudmouth drunk and bully who claimed to relish the idea of going home to persecute Fenians. He had been promoted to lance-corporal several times, but each time had lost his stripe for fighting while drunk. He was stocky and intimidating and tried to give the impression that nothing would give him greater pleasure than to shoot a Catholic. He would often say to me: "Hiya, Fenian!" I would tell him to fuck off, which would make him laugh. "Ha! Ha! Ha!" he would cackle, as if we were best friends joshing. I hated the bastard.

Another was nicknamed Charisma (because he did not have any). He was about 23 but, with his moustache and boring manner, could have passed for 50. He was the non-smoking, non-drinking "saved" type. His "dah", a UDR man, was a disciple of the Reverend Ian Paisley. Charisma was full of himself and slagged off anyone who didn't share his fundamentalist Protestant beliefs: there were the doomed and the saved, the righteous and the unrighteous, and I knew which category he put me in. Once I was lying on my bed trying to sleep while listening to him droning on about God and republicans and loyalty to the Queen.

Finally I snapped and shouted: "Shut the fuck up, you lemon." In our regiment "lemon" was slang for a yellow (that is, gutless) Orangeman.

He was holding his rifle which he had been cleaning. He leant over my bed, pointed it at me and said: "Bang! Bang! You fucking Fenian."

I jumped out of bed and he ran off. I had no respect for people like Nasty and Charisma. They were full of hatred for people they had never spoken to or listened to. They sounded like they were parroting what their "dahs" had told them: bigots breeding bigots. I also wondered why, if they were so committed to getting in there and bashing the Fenians, they had not joined the RUC, the UDR or the Paras, rather than a regiment they believed would never visit their beloved homeland. When in their company I often felt that if I'd been brought up a Catholic alongside them I would probably have ended up stalking the countryside with black balaclava and Kalashnikov hoping to shoot them.

I made the mistake a few times of trying to have an argument with them about Northern Ireland. I had no real interest in the politics of the situation – quite frankly, it bored me – but I had the gut feeling, shared by most English, Welsh and even Scottish squaddies, that the six counties belonged to Ireland. When the loyalists said that Northern Ireland was (and always would be) British my argument was (and still is): "It's like saying London doesn't belong to the English." But you couldn't argue with them, because they wouldn't put forward any reasoned arguments. They would just bluster and shout and tell you that even to question the link with Great Britain was tantamount to treachery.

One time when Charisma told me that his ancestors, with God's help, had settled the land I drove him to a fury by telling him that when I had done thieving in the past I'd at least had the decency not to walk round saying that God had given me permission to do it and was happy for me to keep the spoils.

Not all of the regiment's Ulster Protestants shared the same attitudes. In fact, someone I got on well with was Mac from Derry. I never heard him utter a single word against Catholics and, if anything, he regarded extremist loyalists like Nasty and Charisma with even more disdain than I did. Mac was heavily built and, like me, lacked two front teeth, although in his case their absence did not hinder his ability to wolf down huge quantities of food. Like me, he hated the spit-and-polish army bullshit. He had enlisted because of the limited job opportunities in Derry. He had thought that by choosing "the Skins" (our regiment's nickname) he would not be called to serve in Northern Ireland. Like most squaddies, he was fond of a drink and, like me, he was not shy when violence, or the potential for it, presented itself.

I arrived at St Angelo as Bobby Sands seemed to be nearing the end of his hunger strike. He had done more than 50 days.

I suppose for the first few weeks no-one was convinced he would die: everyone expected a last-minute intervention from some quarter. But as he headed towards the 60-day mark people were sure he would go through with it. Soldiers tried to hide their anxiety about the consequences of Sands's death by making a joke of it. Apart from the "Slimmer of the Year" captions that covered the camp there was also a Hunger Strike Sweepstake: on a board in the operations room were listed the names of all republicans on hunger strike. Soldiers would have to guess the number of days a particular hunger striker would take to die. Each guess cost one pound and the soldier who guessed correctly would get to keep the pot.

But in those first few days at St Angelo the Hunger Strike was not uppermost in my mind. I had a more personal concern, namely, the agony being caused to me by piles – a common problem for soldiers near the border where everywhere you sat was either damp or cold. I could hardly walk or sleep: the back of my lightweight army trousers was covered in blood. I felt a little embarrassed and at first tried to bear my ailment uncomplainingly in the hope it would disappear.

One of my first shifts was on a permanent VCP near the border. When the helicopter dropped us off I found the VCP had been built on and around an old pig sty: soldiers used the troughs as beds. Everything stank. After a while I decided I could bear my condition no longer. I got on the radio to base. A female voice answered at the other end. I assumed she was one of the UDR Greenfinches who worked in the operations room. I explained my predicament and asked her to arrange for haemorrhoid cream to be sent to relieve my inflamed anus. I said: "I can't walk, I can't sleep and I look like I've been shot in the arse." I tried to get her to make the cream an urgent military priority. She laughed and said she would do what she could. Periodically I would get back on the radio to see if a special helicopter mission had been launched to save me. It became a big joke. However, I got what I wanted: the next helicopter dropped off the cream.

Everyone did 12-hour shifts: if you were not manning VCPs you were out on patrol or on guard duty at the camp. I did one guard duty, but found it so tedious that from then on I would swap my guard shifts with soldiers who had been rostered for patrol duty. After your shift you would try to get some sleep in a room with 20 others. There was never silence: soldiers were always coming and going, but the greatest enemy of sleep, if not mental stability, was the room's cassette-player. On it, 24-hours-a-day, every day, was played the one and only tape – Phil Collins's first album, *Face Value*. I soon knew every word of every song on that LP. The drum solo on "In the Air Tonight" still haunts me today. Indeed, when any of those songs comes on the radio I feel ill.

I can't remember where exactly I was when Bobby Sands died on the 66th day of his fast, but I remember the moment the news came through. I was on a mobile patrol which we had set up on the outskirts of a predominantly nationalist town. Someone had devised a special code in preparation for the event. It was something like, "Grey Fox has left." I was near the radio operator when the words came over the airwaves. Everyone in the patrol knew within seconds and everyone looked worried: we knew his death could only spell trouble – and we still had more than three months to do. Shortly afterwards, as if to underline our fears, people from houses a few hundred yards away came out onto the streets and started banging dustbin lids on the ground. Everyone was on edge. Even the motorists we stopped that night seemed more bolshy and aggressive. I felt relieved when the helicopter came to take us back to camp.

Bobby Sands's death and the crowd of 70,000 at his subsequent funeral added to the atmosphere of fear and paranoia at St Angelo. Every nationalist area in Fermanagh seemed covered with black flags and memorial posters. This widespread sympathy for the dead Provo confirmed the prejudices of people like Nasty and Charisma that all Catholics were closet republicans. The locally-recruited UDR soldiers with whom we shared the camp felt the same. In the canteen and bar they would talk as if an uprising were imminent. I often heard UDR people say, "Kill all Catholics. Let God sort them out." But behind their bravado I could smell fear – fear of the growing strength of the IRA, both on the ground and in terms of the international support the Hunger Strike was attracting for the republican movement. Some UDR people seemed to be anticipating the day when they and their families would be slaughtered in their beds by the rampaging Fenian hordes.

Everyone was jumpy. We were reminded never to accept gifts from people at VCPs. There were various horror stories of how republicans had ground down lightbulbs and then put the glass powder in bottles of soft drinks to be given to thirsty soldiers; or how soldiers had accepted a portable television from a kindly motorist only to have it explode when they turned it on. You had to remember that everyone you met might potentially be out to kill you. This awareness of being surrounded by hidden threats put a great strain on all our minds and I could see some soldiers beginning to crack, especially the younger ones. You had to be 18 to qualify for service in Northern Ireland. There was one soldier nicknamed Foxy who had only moved into technical adulthood a fortnight before the start of our tour. He was small and slight with mousy features and a nervous manner. From the moment he knew we were being sent to Ireland he pestered me. I suppose he latched on to me because we were both from the Black Country – I from near Wolverhampton, he from West Bromwich. In Fermanagh he pestered me even more. He would say things like: "Do you think there's going to be a lot more trouble if more hunger strikers die?" I would think the answer reasonably obvious and would say yes. Foxy would then dispute what I'd said. In fact I don't know why he ever asked me anything. I never told him what he needed to hear – I would always tell him the worst – and then he would disagree with me. We were usually told the night before where we would be going on patrol the next day. Once we knew the location Foxy would invariably seek me out and engage me in the same conversation, night after night. It usually went something like this:

"What d'you think about this, O'Mahoney?"

"Think about what?"

"Where we're going tomorrow. Is it really bad there?"

"I don't know."

"What do you think? Do you think it's really bad there?"

"How the fuck do I know?"

"They reckon it's bad there..."

He was a master of the unanswerable question. He began to drive me round the bend, so I started taking revenge by winding him up. The more nervous he got, the more I would wind him up. One day we talked about the possibility of being separated from your "brick" and being captured by the enemy. In training we had been told that if we were unable to shoot our way out then we ought to consider shooting ourselves: capture would lead to unimaginable horrors, at the end of which the only certainty was death. This thought preyed on Foxy's mind. We discussed it one night – and many nights thereafter. In fact we had so many similar conversations that I can remember his ramblings almost word for word:

"Would you shoot yourself if that happened, O'Mahoney?"

"Fucking right I would, Foxy."

"No you wouldn't. You're just saying that."

"All right then, I wouldn't. I'd let them beat me, torture me, hack off my remaining bollock and then shoot me."

"No you wouldn't." Pause. "What sort of things do you think they'd do?"

"How the fuck do I know?"

"Do you think they'd use weapons on you or just beat you?"

"Foxy. I do not fucking know."

"Have they ever let anyone go?"

"No."

"Well, perhaps it would be better to shoot yourself, then." Pause. Then: "How would you know they were for real, though? What if they weren't really the IRA and..."

And on and on he would gibber into the night, torturing himself, and me, with his dark thoughts. I said to him once that the Provos would soon regret capturing him: he would bore them to death with his questions. He could really work himself into a state. I began to see that the biggest threat to soldiers in Northern Ireland came from the workings of their own minds. It was, more than anything else, a psychological conflict.

But of course there were real threats. Sometimes the faceless terrorists could be given names. At that time the most feared IRA man in our area was James Lynagh. He lived over the border and was considered so dangerous that the security forces gave him his own code name. There were lots of stories about his daredevil cunning, such as how he would hide in car boots which he would spring open as he passed police stations to open fire with a machine-gun. He must have been under surveillance by the southern Irish Special Branch because whenever he went on the missing list a warning would come on the radio: "Bill has left the stage," or something like that. If he had gone missing everyone assumed he had crossed the border and that an attack was imminent. If you were at a permanent checkpoint when those words came over the radio you couldn't help feeling a little spooked. You would be sitting in your sandbag sangar 100 yards away from everyone else and your mind would start playing games with you. Any movement in the darkness in front of you would be terrifying. You could not see what was making the noise so you assumed it was James Lynagh.

The VCP would be surrounded by trip wires armed with flares at night – disarmed during the day. If a flare went off you would automatically want to open fire. However, the intruders were always animals. It was in an incident like that around that time that I shot my first sheep. In fact, soldiers often accidentally shot sheep or rabbits or foxes or even, occasionally, cows. In fact, no animal was safe, especially if paratroopers were on duty. Sometimes we used to share a VCP with 2 Para. They were different from us, more professional, which in military terms meant they just wanted to kill things, people preferably, but any animal would do. Once we were sharing a

VCP near a farm with members of 2 Para. The farm dog would start barking whenever soldiers changed guard and moved from the sleeping quarters to the machine-gun post. The paras decided that the dog's barking would alert terrorists to the movement of soldiers when they were at their most vulnerable. So a para crawled into the farm and silenced the dog for good with a knife.

As for James Lynagh – he was part of an eight-man IRA unit wiped out by the SAS at Loughgall six years later. The RUC claimed that weapons recovered from the bodies had been used in seven murders and nine attempted murders in the previous two years.

Other strange things would happen at night when the darkness could provide cover for our antics. Around the time Bobby Sands died we tended to feel safer back at base. One evening I was on a mobile patrol roving through the countryside around Belcoo. It had been raining in that special Irish way since we had first jumped off the helicopter. Everyone was soaked. Most depressingly, all our sleeping bags were soaked, which meant that if we had to set up temporary camp we would not even be able to have the comfort of a warm sleeping bag (our "green maggot", as it was known) for a short snooze. Our corporal was equally dejected.

We decided to have a false "contact". If you encountered terrorists while on patrol and opened fire you were supposed to get on the radio immediately and shout "Contact! Contact! Contact!" That night's Quick Reaction Force would then be despatched to you swiftly by helicopter as back-up. But, most importantly, as your position had been compromised you would have to be taken back to camp to your nice warm bed and a cup of tea. We all agreed on our story in case there was an investigation: we had spotted a figure who appeared to be carrying a rifle near a tree several hundred yards away. I laughed as we took up firing positions. Then, at the corporal's command, we fired off two flares and opened fire on the tree and bushes. The sky lit up like it was Fireworks Night and the machine-gunner blasted countless rounds of tracer bullets into the tree and bushes, while we added to the show with bullets from our SLRs. Meanwhile the corporal was screaming into the radio handset: "Contact! Contact! Contact!"

Back at base they must have thought we'd encountered an IRA Flying Column. Within seven minutes we heard the whirr of the helicopter. Soldiers jumped from it before it had even touched the ground. They ran towards us, hyped up and ready for action. Our corporal pointed in the direction of the tree and the QRF soldiers moved off to hunt down the enemy, helped by the helicopter's powerful search beam. When we got back to base I could tell that some of the officers suspected something, but nothing was said. I think they put our reaction down to nervousness.

And everyone was nervous. Within days our regiment had its second casualty. A soldier was shot in the foot. Thankfully, he hadn't been shot by other soldiers – he'd shot himself. At the front of St Angelo were two watchtowers near the main gate. I was on QRF duty when the call came that there had been a shooting incident in one of the watchtowers. I ran with the others the few hundred yards to the tower and climbed to the top of the steps where I could see a soldier lying on the floor surrounded by five or six others who were shouting at him. When I got closer I could see a perfect hole in one of the prone soldier's boots. The boot was still on his foot and there was remarkably little blood. The soldier was not saying anything, just lying there rigid, his face drained of colour. He was obviously in shock, but the other soldiers were giving him abuse, rather than sympathy. Someone kept screaming: "What the fuck have you done? What the fuck have you done?" They eventually put him on a stretcher and carried him to a helicopter which flew him to hospital. Later he claimed the gun had gone off accidentally while he was sitting with his foot up.

He might have been telling the truth, but no-one believed him.

12

Contact! Contact! Contact!

BOBBY SANDS died on the Tuesday. The Fermanagh Provos took their revenge on the Saturday.

I was lying on my bed in our sleeping quarters, reading someone else's tabloid newspaper. The other members of that night's Quick Reaction Force were either lying on their beds or sitting in twos and threes around the room, talking quietly and seriously. Bobby Sands's death and our thoughts about its possible consequences had removed all lightness from the atmosphere. Everyone expected something unpleasant just around the corner. Phil Collins, as always, provided the background music: ". . . coming in the air tonight, oh Lord, oh, Loooorrddd. . ." It was around 10.30 p.m., too early to bother trying to sleep. I half expected we'd get called out at some point that night. I imagined the local republicans getting tanked up in the pubs to mark the passing of their MP. They would soon be spilling out onto the streets looking for targets they could vent their anger on.

I threw the newspaper down and sat up just as the door flew open. A soldier shouted: "Heli-pad! Heli-pad! They've attacked Rosslea!" We burst into activity, grabbing our weapons and running out the door into the slumbering camp. A few hundred yards away on the heli-pad I could see the rotors of the Lynx in full frenetic spin. I threw myself into the helicopter and huddled down in the seat behind the pilot. Within seconds everyone was aboard and the Lynx lifted up smoothly. Then, as it passed the roofs of the watchtowers, a powerful thrust from the engine sent the sleek machine zooming off into the darkness.

"Mortar attack. Rosslea," shouted the brick commander. I felt my stomach slipping an inch – I knew almost all the soldiers at Rosslea, although I had no close friends there. It was one of the smallest and most vulnerable camps, usually described as a joint RUC/Army base. In fact it was little more than an old police station based in what looked like a normal four-bedroom family house with four Portakabins in the garden. A barbed wire fence surrounded the camp, which stood alone, apart from a pig farm next door. I had been there a few times and each time had felt relieved to get back to St Angelo, which by comparison was an impregnable fortress. The person I knew best at Rosslea was Edwards, a Catholic from Liverpool. I had been through basic training with him and liked him. He was quiet, tending to keep himself to himself, but he could be a good laugh. I felt anxious for him and hoped he was not now "fertiliser" – our slang for the dead victims of explosions.

The pilot was in contact with Rosslea and through the information he relayed to our brick commander I could tell the base was in total panic. People were shouting and screaming down the radio. I looked out of the window. At first I could see nothing, only blackness, but within a few minutes an orange glow appeared in the distance. As we got closer the glow got bigger until I could clearly make out flames. The atmosphere in the helicopter was full of fear and tension. In no time at all we were there and, as the helicopter circled, we found ourselves looking down on a scene of devastation. The whole camp seemed alight: orange and yellow flames danced madly around plumes of grey-black smoke. I could make out figures running around the flames. I felt a dryness in my mouth and a sickness in my stomach. The pilot was looking for a safe spot to land: he had to be careful – we had been told there were unexploded mortars on the ground. As the helicopter hovered I watched the scene below with horrified fascination. I knew there had to be casualties. Surely the Provos could not blast the camp apart like that and not hit anyone? I felt almost hypnotised by the mayhem. In that half-trance part of me was expecting the professionals to arrive to sort things out. Then the reality hit me: we were the professionals – we were the ones the people on the ground were waiting for to sort things out.

The helicopter landed in a field opposite the base. For a second I felt as if I could not move, but as the others started to jump out I forced myself up. The Lynx lifted off as soon as the last person had jumped out. I don't think any of us knew what we were going to do. We all ran towards a hole in the fence, which had bits of Portakabin hanging off it. Groups of soldiers had gathered just inside the perimeter, away from the flames. Everyone looked dazed and shocked. Nearby I saw one group kneeling over a figure stretched out on the ground.

I said to one: "What the fuck's happening?"

He said: "Mortars. Some haven't gone off."

I asked if anyone was hurt.

He said: "Edwards." He pointed to the figure on the ground.

I felt sick as I ran to where he was lying. The others beside him seemed to be too shocked to do anything. I knelt down beside them and could hardly recognise the prone figure as Edwards. He was shaking and making gibbering noises, but what struck me most at first glance was how dirty he was: his face and clothes were covered in filth. Then I noticed his wounds. There was a gash on his face, starting on his cheek and stretching down past the jaw, but most sickeningly his right side had been ripped open. Blood was oozing out of the wound, which must have stretched for about 18 inches down his side and into his back.

I said: "Where's the first aid kit?"

I was told they could not find it: everything had been blown away. Even the electricity was off: the only light came from the flames. Edwards, barely conscious, was just shaking with shock. I thought: "Fuck. He's going to die." I shouted for them to get some bandages or something – anything – which I could use to press down on the wounds to try to stem the blood flow. Someone ran over to the wreckage and came back with something. He handed me several pairs of clean socks. I started pressing them into the wounds. Soon Edwards was lying there with socks hanging out of his side and face. I asked if they had called the emergency services. They said the fire brigade was on its way, but the ambulance service would not come out this far.

I said: "We've got to get the helicopter back to get him to hospital."

The QRF's sergeant, who had initially been speechless with shock, got on the radio. Edwards started gibbering manically.

"Calm down! Calm down! It's me, Bernie," I said. I was shocked to see my friend in such a state. I kept saying: "Clarkey, Clarkey. You're all right. Stop moaning." Why I called him Clarke – the name of another soldier I'd met at Sutton Coldfield selection centre – I shall never know. I was terrified he was dying in front of me.

Another sergeant was telling everyone to get out of the camp and to take up firing positions in the field: he was worried about unexploded mortars and the possibility of a follow-up attack. I and a few others insisted on staying with Edwards. The QRF sergeant was having an argument with the helicopter pilot, who was saying it was too dangerous to land. Our sergeant started screaming down the mouthpiece at him until he relented. The pilot said he would not land too near the camp: he suggested a spot in the middle of a nearby field. During this time someone had managed to find a stretcher. We put Edwards on it and wound a ragged blanket around his body to hold in the socks. We picked up the stretcher and ran with it through the hole in the fence. We watched the helicopter circling and heard the reassuring DUB-DUB-DUB-DUB-DUB of its rotors as it dipped down towards us. As we ran we saw the helicopter almost touch the ground a few hundred yards away. It hovered a few feet off the ground, waiting for its cargo. As we ran we could not help bouncing Edwards in the stretcher. He shouted out in pain.

To our frustration there was a ditch and a hedge between us and the helicopter. I told four of the others to jump over the hedge and be ready to receive the stretcher. They climbed over the hedge and found themselves on raised ground. By this time Edwards was moaning: "Ooooooooohhhhhhh!!" The rest of us stood in the ditch and lifted up the stretcher. Those on the other side grabbed one end of it and pulled. Unfortunately, none of us noticed that the ragged blanket had got caught in the hedge. So when they pulled the stretcher free and started running with it the trapped blanket held on to Edwards – and catapulted him back into the ditch on top of us. Meanwhile the others, perhaps in shock, were still running towards the waiting helicopter with the empty stretcher. As three of us lay in a heap in the ditch with Edwards on top of us moaning even louder than before I burst out laughing. This farce amid the horror had set me off. The stretcher-bearers soon realised they had lost their patient and came running back. They threw over the stretcher as we disentangled ourselves and stood up. We put Edwards back on the stretcher and passed it over again. This time he stayed with the stretcher.

I watched as they ran to the helicopter and placed the stretcher inside. The helicopter lifted off and disappeared into the darkness.

At that moment I felt a powerful hatred for the Provos. Edwards was a good man: he didn't deserve to die. I dearly hoped I'd get a chance to kill one of the bastards who had done that to him. We ran back to the camp. Everyone had taken up firing positions outside the perimeter fence, but well away from some unexploded mortars which lay smouldering in one of the fields. Within ten minutes several fire engines had arrived. They had powerful lights which enabled us to see more clearly as we were now some way from the dying flames. The firemen unreeled their hoses but, as they turned on the water, some ammunition stored in one of the Portakabins started going off. The bullets made a DO-DO-DO-DO-DO sound. The firemen must have assumed that the Provos had launched a follow-up attack, because as soon as they heard the bullets they dropped the hoses, jumped into their fire engines and drove off, hoses trailing behind them, spewing water all over the road.

Our sergeant screamed: "Get those fuckers back here! Get them back!" But it was too late – they had disappeared into the night.

Within 20 minutes the fire had almost burnt itself out and we were in pitch darkness. Instead of staying put, the sergeant said we had to clear the area to create a safe cordon all round the camp. We advanced slowly through the field.

Suddenly I heard a soldier shout: "Halt! Who goes there?"

There was no reply. We crouched down and pointed our rifles in front of us. I could feel my heart pounding. Was this the Provo who had got Edwards? Was this the bastard? If it was, he was going to die – the crate of beer would be mine. I noticed a movement just ahead of us.

Someone shouted again: "Who goes there?" Still no reply. After a short pause we got up and began advancing slowly towards the figure, fingers on triggers. We surrounded it – and it suddenly ran at us. I don't know why none of us started shooting; I myself was within a millisecond of pulling the trigger. That sheep would never know how close it had come to losing its life.

We stayed in the fields until first light. As we waited for the sun to come up I spoke to a soldier who had been in the camp during the attack. He said that by a miraculous fluke almost all the soldiers, except for Edwards, had been in the one Portakabin that had escaped unscathed.

In the morning the fire brigade returned and hosed down the smouldering Portakabins. Then the bomb-disposal people arrived. A short way from the camp I could see the lorry from which the mortars had been fired: a three-ton Bedford with ten firing tubes on the back. Apparently, only three mortars had hit the base. Those three had been accurate because they had been the first to be fired. However, they had shot off with such force that the pressure had broken the lorry's back suspension. This had altered the trajectory of the other mortars, all of which had missed their target. One had even landed in the pig farm next door.

Once the area had been declared safe a helicopter landed to bring more troops and to take us back to St Angelo.

13

Welcome to Botswana

IT WAS hard to get any news of Edwards. The army tried to stop us dwelling on the misfortunes of our comrades, presumably to stop morale sinking even lower. "He's all right. Forget about him." was the official attitude, one that I'd come across before in Germany. Naturally, it achieved the opposite of what was intended: we only dwelled more on the fate of our injured friend – and rumours filled the vacuum created by the lack of information. One of the most bizarre things that would happen after such an incident was the stripping of the injured person's bed: they would remove everything – sheets, blankets and even the mattress. Sometimes the first you knew that something had happened was when you returned to the bare bed-springs in the bunk above you. You didn't know what had happened, but you assumed it wasn't good. Within a few days of the mortar attack there was even the rumour that Edwards had died – and been secretly buried to maintain morale. However, by the end of the week, with persistent questioning, we'd managed to establish that Edwards's condition was stable. He was expected to make a full recovery.

In a strange way the Provos' attack helped settle nerves a little. It provided a weird reassurance: we had been anticipating something awful, so when it happened it confirmed we were right to have expected the worst. Not that any of us thought we had yet experienced the worst. We could see the republican prisoners chugging along the starvation conveyor belt – and we knew their friends on the outside would be looking to avenge each one that came to the end of the line.

On the surface people tried to treat the Hunger Strike as a joke, usually by making quips about the regimental sweepstake, but among friends huddled in smaller groups most people would be more circumspect. Soldiers rarely admitted openly to being afraid, but fear was all around. We would discuss the news and hope that none of the soon-to-be-deceased would be buried in Fermanagh: Provo funerals could only mean trouble. Outside the company of trusted friends, and especially in the presence of UDR soldiers, many would join in the celebratory sneering at the impending deaths of republican prisoners. Indeed, when the next hunger striker died most people in the canteen started cheering. The 25-year-old IRA man Francis Hughes went within a week of Bobby Sands after starving himself for 59 days. Once again sympathisers came onto the streets to bang dustbin lids on the ground. In the canteen I heard one UDR man suggest that the army ought to raid Catholic areas and confiscate all dustbin lids for the duration of the Hunger Strike. I think he was serious.

We all turned into news junkies, eagerly congregating in the television room to catch the news bulletins. The whole of Northern Ireland seemed to be erupting during this period. In Belfast masked youths stoned and petrol-bombed the security forces, set up roadblocks and set vehicles ablaze. A soldier was shot in the chest when his foot patrol came under fire in West Belfast. We tutted in disgust when the reporter said the rest of the patrol had been unable to return fire because of the civilians milling around. Soldiers shouted at the TV screen: "Shoot them all, the bastards." In Dungannon a police patrol was ambushed with petrol bombs. In Newry a car showroom went up in flames. The camera panned across the smouldering cars. In the TV room a soldier got a laugh by saying: "Shit! I'd put a deposit on that one."

Out on patrol I remember feeling puzzled by the huge number of small black mourning flags flying from lamp-posts, houses, pubs and other businesses. I thought people were foolish to advertise their loyalty to the IRA in that way. To my criminal mind it seemed as absurd as the idea of my sticking a poster in my front-room window at home saying, "Dear Police. I am a criminal. Please arrest me." Yet at the same time part of me admired what I saw as the flag-wavers' come-and-get-me defiance of the authorities. We took note of who was flying the flag – and we intended coming to get them if we had time to get round to them all. I am sure the RUC, UDR and loyalist paramilitaries thought the same. In briefings we were warned not to try to pull down the flags in case they were booby-trapped. We had to be content with setting fire to a few of them. There was even a report of loyalists firing gunshots at black flags in Maguiresbridge. I thought it was probably some of the UDR men on a works outing.

I remember another briefing around this time when a sergeant told us that republicans were now throwing acid bombs as well as petrol bombs – milk bottles full of sulphuric acid. The thought of acid eating into my skin horrified me more than the thought of being engulfed in flames. The sergeant said that if anyone was hit with an acid bomb we had to rinse him thoroughly with water as soon as possible. It seemed to me that the acid would have done its corrosive work by the time any rinsing took place. Nevertheless, we started making sure we never left camp without filling our water bottles to the brim.

The rioters were devising more and more ingeniously vicious ways of causing us damage. Just as you could trace the Provos' developments in mortar-bomb technology (the Mark One turning into the more sophisticated Mark Two turning into the more sophisticated Mark Three and so on) you could also trace developments in petrol-bomb technology. We were told they had started putting balls of elastic bands into bottles. The burning petrol would cause the elastic to melt into a thick blob of goo. If the rioters scored a direct hit on a soldier or policeman this goo would stick to the victim, impossible to shake off, burning furiously as it melted into flesh or clothing. In the first few weeks of the tour we had been allowed to carry carbon-dioxide fire extinguishers with us for use in petrol-bomb attacks. They worked on the principle of extinguishing a fire by starving the flames of oxygen. However, the instruction came through that we were not to use the extinguishers on burning colleagues. Apparently a soldier in Belfast had almost died when his mates had used one on him when his uniform had caught fire during a riot. The carbon dioxide had starved the soldier, as well as the flames, of oxygen and he had come close to suffocating.

The canteen was a lively place during the day. The duty cooks would be crashing about, washing the steel trays or moving the steel pots and steel pans from steel surface to steel surface. Soldiers would sit in groups of four or five; events would dictate their mood and conversation. A lot was said among the cannon-fodder which would not have been aired in the company of officers or those we regarded as "real" soldiers.

A regular topic of conversation was the number of days you had to do before R and R (Rest and Recuperation). The latter was the three days' special leave you were granted for being in Northern Ireland. Only a few soldiers would be on R and R at the same time. Some got theirs after only a week in the country, while others had to wait until the last fortnight of the tour. Many soldiers had "days-to-do" charts pinned beside their beds next to the A3-size Page-Three pin-ups sent by *The Sun* to "Our Brave Boys". The charts marked the day of arrival to the day of supposed departure: R and R days would be highlighted with shades from fluorescent marker pens. Those who seemed to pine most for the day when they could put a cross through the last date were usually the ones making the jokes about the regimental sweepstake. They made me sick.

By late evening the canteen would be a much quieter place where you could seek refuge from others. There would still be two cooks on duty, washing up, preparing food or making urns of the ever-available tea. By the early hours there was rarely more than a handful of soldiers sitting around, usually members of patrols that had just come in or were about to go out. Soldiers tended not to talk much at those times: either they were too tired to bother or too immersed in their thoughts of what awaited them on their next trip outside the camp.

The canteen was sometimes used for a show – two strippers and a comedian whose career had probably peaked 20 years earlier. Usually the only people who got to see the shows were the Rear Echelon Mother Fuckers. Most of the other squaddies would be either on guard duty, manning VCPs, out on patrol or sleeping. Not that they missed much. I went to one – and regretted going as soon as I sat down. The presence of officers had sucked from the atmosphere any potential for fun. With them there we were expected to behave with discipline and restraint, so the raunchy show supposedly designed to take a young man's mind off the horrors of Ulster for a few hours usually failed to achieve its artistic purpose. At the one I attended the lowest point came when one of the strippers, the marginally more animated one, dangled her breasts over an officer's face and the audience applauded politely. Boredom drove me back to my bunk for an early night.

In the main the recreation was in the bar, a pokey but tolerable place with a dance floor and tables and chairs for up to 80 people. Even there you were expected to behave in a disciplined and restrained manner. You were not supposed to have more than three pints, even though you were off-duty. The bar staff had the job of monitoring and regulating your intake. Of course I broke that rule, like I broke all the others, but you didn't have to be a criminal mastermind to work your way around it – you just got the more sensible non-drinkers to go to the bar for you. A lot of soldiers who had been fond of drink in Germany avoided it at St Angelo in order to be fully sober at all times in case the Provos tried to storm the camp. Mac, I and a few others had a more relaxed attitude: we often emerged from that bar very well pissed, having drunk our own, and several other soldiers', alcohol quotas.

The bar's most regular inhabitants were off-duty UDR men: it was probably the only place in Fermanagh where they felt they could drink safely. Friday and Saturday nights were the busiest in the bar. A DJ would come in and the UDR soldiers would bring in their families. At first I didn't have too much to do with the UDR men, but I soon became interested in one of the UDR women. She was slim with long raven-black hair. In that male-dominated environment she attracted a lot of attention. I managed to get talking to her one night when she came to the bar with a few of the other Greenfinches from the operations room. She said her name was Elizabeth and she soon recognised my voice as that of the soldier who had been making the urgent requests for cream to ease his piles. Apparently, I had caused a lot of amusement in the ops room. She asked me if the cream had arrived safely. I said it had and asked her if she would let me say thank-you to the ops room Greenfinches by buying her a drink. Over the following weeks as we spent more time together in the bar we drifted into a relationship. It was very romantic: my piles had brought us together.

On 13 May 1981, only a day after Francis Hughes's death, someone shot the Pope in Rome, seriously wounding him. This attempted assassination became the talk of the camp, especially among the fundamentalist Protestants, who were hugely disappointed by the gunman's failure to kill the Anti-Christ. I heard people like Nasty and Charisma debating the incident as they would a vital goal that had been disallowed at a cup final:

if only the stupid bastard had shot him in the head or if only he had used a different weapon. Groups of UDR men pored over newspaper reports in the canteen, bitterly criticising the would-be assassin's failings. Religion was an irrelevance to me, and I had not been to church in years, yet at the same time I still regarded myself as a Catholic, if only in name. I couldn't blame the Ulster Protestants for hating Irish republicans, but I didn't like the way their hatred seemed to cover every member of the Catholic Church, regardless of nationality. Edwards, who had just been wounded, was a Catholic. It was one of those moments when I felt distanced from these people, although I wore the same uniform. I felt no sense of loyalty to them and certainly didn't see myself as fighting for them.

But the six counties were not short of narrow-minded Catholics either. In early May all soldiers on patrol or at checkpoints had been given the details of a Fermanagh musician who had apparently gone missing while on a trip to Dublin. He had formed a heavy rock band called "Mama's Boys", although his parents had been long associated with the traditional Irish music scene. We thought he wouldn't be seen alive again, expecting his body to turn up at a border crossing with a bag over his head – the usual outcome when someone from the north went missing on a trip to the south. However, after a few days he turned up alive. The following week I read in the local paper that his captors had sent a letter to journalists saying they had detained the man because his group had "left Irish traditional music to play nigger junk". It was signed "Irish Traditional Purists". In my mind the words "nationalists", "republicans", "unionists", and "loyalists" just represented one set of mad bastards fighting another set of mad bastards. Most of the time I felt they could live in this madhouse slaughtering each other for all eternity. I just wanted to make sure that in the process they didn't slaughter me or anyone I cared about.

I suppose a complicating factor was that I was beginning to care about Elizabeth. Not hugely – I wasn't a falling-in-love sort of person – but enough to start viewing things at times in a different way, one that was not entirely hostile to the indigenous tribes. Elizabeth was shy and gentle and didn't speak with hatred of anyone. She came from a family that was well-known and respected within the area. Most members of her family were involved in one way or another in defending the northern Irish part of Her Majesty's realm. Her father and brother were policemen and she said her mother was active in the Democratic Unionist Party. I looked blank when she told me – I didn't have much of a clue about local politics – but she helped me clarify what the DUP stood for when she said it was the party led by the Reverend Ian Paisley. Apparently, the Official Unionists were the other, bigger unionist party and they were not led by Paisley.

Elizabeth told me her mother was campaigning to be elected onto the local council. She gave me one of her campaign leaflets for the May elections. The photo showed a well-groomed matron staring sternly. In the blurb Elizabeth's mother said she solemnly promised, among other things, to "stand against any sell out of Northern Ireland" and "to speak out on moral issues affecting society". The leaflet urged electors to "vote for the unionist party you can trust – Democratic Unionists (DUP). SERVICE EVER – SURRENDER NEVER." The rest of it was taken up with an attack on the rival Official Unionists, although it referred to people and events of whom and of which I was almost wholly ignorant:

An Answer to Powell, Molyneaux etc
WHO???
Handed over the "B" Specials;
Voted away the Stormont Parliament;
Accepted the Sunningdale Agreement;
Shared Power with Republicans;
Avoided voting for a Stormont Parliament;
Agreed with the Government's Security;
Destroyed the Loyalist Coalition;
Wrecked the UUUC;
Ruined Fermanagh/S. Tyrone Unionist Unity;
Called the election that suited the IRA;
Laughed at the Toome Loyalist farmers;
Co-operated with Éire Councillors;
Asked for items on the Dublin Talks agenda;
Used the Pope for electioneering;
Mocked morality and the Lord Jesus Christ:
THE OFFICIAL UNIONISTS!

I could see where Elizabeth had got her traditional values from.

I remember those May elections for the way we set out to harass candidates standing in support of the hunger strikers. We would stop and search them and their supporters whenever possible and generally try to disrupt their campaign in whatever petty ways presented themselves. Not that we had much effect: they still managed to strengthen their position on Fermanagh District Council, taking four seats. Elizabeth's mother came bottom of the poll in her area. Elsewhere in Northern Ireland H-Block candidates picked up another 32 seats, getting 51,000 votes in total.

There was one would-be politician whom we tormented

mercilessly for months. His name was Owen Carron. He had been the election agent of the hunger striker and MP Bobby Sands and he subsequently became the republicans' candidate in the parliamentary by-election following Sands's death. The election was due to be held on the second last day of our tour in August 1981. I first saw him outside Enniskillen library, a small bearded man with an intense look. He was ranting through a grey loud-hailer at a small crowd. In briefings at St Angelo I remember officers telling us he was a teacher. For some reason this made him even more of a bogeyman for us. I think we resented the idea that he might be tutoring innocent little children in the ways of terrorism. "Now, Seaneen, when you've done your homework I want you to go out and throw a gob-stopper at one of those Brit bastards." At several of these briefings we were clearly instructed to make life difficult for him – and the order seemed to have come down from on high.

All of us, whenever we got the chance, proceeded to make his life hell. Our pursuit of him was so sustained and relentless that after a while I even began to feel a little sorry for him. One patrol would stop his car, detain him for as long as possible while searching him, let him go, then radio ahead to another patrol who would intercept him and repeat the procedure. He could rarely get more than a few miles without being stopped. If we stopped him on his own in a quiet area we would tell him we were setting him up for assassination by loyalist paramilitaries or threaten to shoot him ourselves. If we stopped his partner in his car we would tell her he was having affairs with other women, that we had caught him with this or that Sinn Féin woman. All lies, of course. Our aim was to hound him into the ground. We wanted to make his life completely

163

miserable – and I think we succeeded. Most of the time he just stood there saying nothing while we took his car apart. But occasionally, very occasionally, he would lose his temper and start shouting – you fucking this, you fucking that. These outbursts would give us great pleasure: we knew we were getting to him. Another element in our pleasure was the bizarre feeling of relief that came from encountering a "known" enemy, someone clearly identifiable in our eyes as a terrorist or terrorist sympathiser. It was as if the spirit of evil that we felt surrounded us at all times had suddenly taken bodily form. And you could get a real rush from confronting the beast.

Some years later, a long time after I had left Northern Ireland, I read in the paper that Carron had gone on the run after being found carrying a rifle in the back of his car. He had probably been looking for me.

It was through Elizabeth that I got to meet so many of the UDR soldiers. By and large, soldiers are quite clannish and tend to keep to the company of their own regimental colleagues, so I didn't expect to be accepted immediately. Several of the UDR people seemed all right, although none of them left me feeling overwhelmed by the desire to form a lifelong friendship. There were, however, several out-and-out bigots who made no attempt to hide their hatred of Catholics. I also noticed that while several of them were friendly enough to me at first they turned cold as soon as they realised my Irish-Catholic origins.

One of the worst bigots was someone I nicknamed Billy Bunter. He was overweight, with a red face, and had the unpleasant habit of sniffing when he finished a sentence. His favourite saying was: "What would really make me happy is if you gave me a pope on a rope." Another of his sayings –

though not uniquely his as it was popular with others – was: "Kill all Catholics. Let God sort them out." He used to boast that his patrol would pick up Catholics in the street for no legitimate reason and, when they begged to be released, would drop them in the middle of loyalist areas. I'd heard of other regiments doing this too. When he found out about my Irish Catholic roots he made a point continually of telling me not to be anywhere near him if a gun battle broke out.

"Yer man," he would say, "Watch your Fenian back if the bullets start flying."

But he was all mouth. I would reply: "Why wait till my back's turned, fat boy?" He would pretend to laugh. Elizabeth told me he had seen one of his relatives shot dead in the street by the IRA. After that I was more tolerant of him, although I still loathed him. It would not have been hard for any of the UDR people to justify their hatred of republicans. Most of them had lost friends or relatives at the hands of the IRA. And all of them, especially the part-timers, lived with a constant sense of personal threat. Out of uniform, at home and at work, they must have felt vulnerable all the time. Behind their backs we used to refer to them as "the Utterly Defenceless Regiment".

On 19 May the IRA killed five soldiers from another regiment, the Royal Green Jackets, when they blew up a Saracen armoured personnel carrier on a country road just outside Newry. The news gave us all a jolt of fear. The TV room at St Angelo was full of soldiers that evening. We watched the report in silence: up to 1,000lbs of explosives had been used in the land mine which had been placed beneath a culvert and detonated by command wire. The explosion had been heard for miles around and had caused power cuts when it severed overhead electricity lines. The solid metal vehicle had been blown to pieces – one of its wheels had been found several hundred yards away, while bits of metal plating had landed in nearby fields. You did not need a vivid imagination to picture what had happened to the Saracen's five occupants. Stories soon circulated that the largest intact piece of body was an arm attached to a shoulder.

Although the attack had taken place well outside our area it still seemed close to home. The countryside there looked exactly like the countryside we were patrolling every day. Around the camp officers tried to treat the incident with indifference. At our first briefing after the attack I remember an officer treating the deaths of these five young men like a bad result at a cricket match – we had lost five, but we would soon even up the score. I was not much given to emotional displays, but even I felt uncomfortable with the lack of humanity in the response.

I read in the paper the statement issued by the Provos' South Armagh Brigade claiming responsibility for the attack. There was one sentence that chilled me: "British soldiers should recognise that the English public and English politicians do not give a damn about the waste of their lives. How many times have you been told that the IRA have been defeated? You are fighting a war you cannot win." It seemed like a personal message to me and confirmed all my most negative feelings. I knew we could not win a war against an invisible enemy and I knew we were just cannon-fodder there to keep things reasonably stable while the politicians worked out what to do. The IRA were right: politicians did not care about those five dead men, any more than they would care about one dead Bernard O'Mahoney. As for the Great British public – they would readily give Ireland back to the Irish for a promise of peace. The only people who would grieve over those mangled bodies were the dead soldiers' families.

"If it could happen to them, it could happen to us," was the unspoken thought in everyone's mind. We all became even more paranoid and fearful whenever we left the camp. I treated everyone, Catholics and Protestants, as a potential threat. Motorists who were nice to me tended to be treated the worst of all. I had the theory that if someone was being nice then they probably had something to hide. Someone who was abusive, on the other hand, was unlikely to have anything in his car because he knew it would be ripped to pieces. I would even turn over English families, because we had been told that there were a lot of English people involved with the Provos. They would stop and I would see on their smiling faces that they were thinking, "Hello! It's our boys here!" Then I would say: "Get out the fucking car." I can still remember the shock and horror on their faces when I treated them like dirt, particularly men who had their wives and children with them. Some would get angry, others would just look hurt, genuinely hurt. One Englishman seemed astonished when I made him empty his car. He said: "But . . . I'm English." On one patrol I stopped a Volkswagen Camper van containing three white Rhodesians. They stopped willingly and were really friendly, congratulating us on the job we were doing. We turned their van upside down, pulling out all their belongings and scattering them over the road. Surprisingly, they maintained their friendliness, even as we body-searched them. Before they drove off one of them offered me a tea towel inscribed with the words, "Welcome to Botswana". I left it in the gutter.

14

Sweeties for the Kiddies

I GREW to love the smell of aviation fuel. Even today when I smell it at airports I find myself thinking of Northern Ireland and those days of travelling everywhere by helicopter.

I usually felt safe inside those noisy wombs, especially at night, when all I could see below were the lights of farmhouses or the headlights of cars as they twisted along border roads. I felt, quite literally, lifted above the troubles. Attacks on helicopters were extremely rare and almost always unsuccessful, so most of the time I could relax and enjoy the view, only being jogged back to paranoid alertness as the pilot zoomed down to the drop zone.

Not all journeys were relaxing. Pilots would sometimes terrorise us with their games. Some Lynx pilots would fly incredibly fast and low, skimming tree tops then turning suddenly to leave us all gasping. Wessex helicopters were heavier and slower, but their pilots would sometimes climb high, then stall the engine, causing the machine to fall rapidly through the air for a few seconds. The effect on your insides was like the one you get in the back-seat of a car going at speed over a hump-back bridge – only 100 times worse. My stomach would rise in my chest and stay there until the pilot bump-started the engine and the machine rose again. The effect was especially devastating if I'd been drinking the night before.

The pilots would often play tricks on civilians as well. Once we were flying low in daylight over Lough Erne. The Wessex pilot spotted a fisherman in a small boat and flew over to him. He positioned the helicopter directly over the boat and hovered there. The down-draught fabricated a mid-Atlantic storm, the waves of which tossed the boat about. The man gesticulated madly, waving his arms desperately until the waves forced him to stoop down and hold on to the side. As he clung on I could see him shouting furiously at us, but the roar of the engines drowned out his words. Inside the helicopter we were all laughing and cheering, hoping his boat would capsize, but before it did so the pilot headed back to St Angelo. Civilians also complained to the local papers about helicopters discharging poisonous substances over their homes. I think these were the by-products of a technique the pilots had for clearing waste from the engines. The pilots would also buzz houses which we had identified as containing republican sympathisers – or people who had annoyed us in some way, perhaps by making complaints. The pilots' favourite trick was to hover longer than necessary over particular houses as they came in to drop us off or pick us up. The down-draught would blow washing off lines, send dustbins flying through the air and generally dislodge anything that was not nailed down. If anyone made an official complaint, the pilot could always justify what he was doing in the area and explain the damage as an accident.

The pilots could drop us anywhere in any conditions. The helicopter would shudder in a distinctive way as it headed towards the ground. As a waterlogged field or peat bog rushed up towards me I would feel my stomach dislodging itself and moving elsewhere. The wheels would barely touch the ground before we leaped out, dashed for cover and sprawled ourselves on the grass in a firing position. A powerful wind from the rotor blades would blow over us as the helicopter lifted off and disappeared. In a few seconds all would be quiet and we would be alone.

On patrol we always had camouflage cream smeared on our faces. It was not the best for skin-care: it left us covered in spots. Patrolling rural areas was an exhausting experience made more arduous by the ban on taking the most obvious route from A to B. We were forbidden to use bridges, gates, stiles or even gaps in hedgerows – places where terrorists might plant booby-traps to catch lazy squaddies. So on even the most apparently straightforward hike we had to scale fences, climb walls, clamber over barbed wire and wade through streams, always loaded down with our backpacks (Bergens) and rifles. We even carried machetes for hacking our way through hedgerows.

We used to carry a special electronic device designed to detect radio-controlled bombs in our path. It looked like a normal transistor radio with a lead connected to an earpiece.

It was meant to give off a special tone if there was a radio-controlled explosive device nearby. Unfortunately, all sorts of innocent things seemed to trigger it off, so in the early days we would be constantly thrown into panic, fleeing in the opposite direction to whatever had caused the warning tone to sound. At times we made the men of *Dad's Army* look like an elite fighting force.

On top of everything certain "objectives" would have been set for us which, more often than not, were impossible to achieve. We would be expected to patrol for miles, checking out numerous farms, small holdings and remote homes. We had been told not to wear water-proofs as they made too much noise, so we would usually be trudging around the fields soaked to the skin. We were supposed to be knocking on doors to ask people questions from a list – names, ages, car registrations, occupations, schools attended by children, religion. I assumed these questionnaires were part of an overall plan to compile a detailed profile of the people living in particular areas. Local republicans complained about an "illegal census" of Catholics being carried out. The army always denied it was carrying out any such systematic census, yet we had been ordered to work our way methodically through areas using the questionnaires. If we were pushed for time, or just feeling lazy, we wouldn't even bother knocking on doors – we'd just enter false details to make it look like we had: "occupants not in", "occupants abusive", "refused to answer door/questions". I have no idea what the intelligence officer collating this material would have recommended for these people. They probably ended up under surveillance or perhaps found themselves thoroughly searched every time they encountered the Crown forces.

Although we concentrated on Catholic areas, we would frequently do Protestant areas too, just to show the natives we were even-handed, which most of us were, at least in the sense that we tried to be unpleasant to everyone equally. I remember on one gloriously sunny day – something unusual in Fermanagh – we went to a staunchly loyalist housing estate, the sort of place where grass was banned for being green and even the dogs were painted red, white and blue. We started knocking on doors with the questionnaires. A middle-aged woman answered my knock. I asked her questions from the list ("Who lives here? Who owns the house? Have you got any sons? Where do they work?").

The woman stared at me with a look of incomprehension. She said: "I'm a Protestant."

I said: "So?"

She began talking to me as if I were a stupid child failing to grasp something obvious: "I don't think you understand. I'm a Protestant."

I said I didn't care what the fuck she was: I wanted her to answer the questions. In those days I never thought there was any point in being polite.

Her face became flushed, her movements agitated. She said I shouldn't be going around bothering good law-abiding Protestant people when there were republican terrorists running around murdering people.

I ignored her and kept asking the questions on the list.

She would not answer them and just kept repeating: "Why are you asking me these questions?"

When she had said this for at least the tenth time I told her to shut the fuck up and answer them. "The sooner you answer them, the sooner I go."

These words sent her into a fury. She called me a foul-mouthed bastard, threatened to report me and told me to go back to England where I belonged. Meanwhile my radio had started making its normal CLLRR-CLRRR sound. She pointed at it and screamed sharply: "You're taping me! You're taping me!"

My corporal ran over from the other side of the road and asked what was happening. By this time the woman was shrieking at me; other neighbours were looking over. The corporal said: "Leave the silly bitch."

I filled in the questionnaire: "Occupant abusive. Refused to answer questions. Possible republican."

We didn't always bring questionnaires. Other times patrols had other aims. An occasional task was the counting of TV aerials. In some streets, without people knowing what we were doing, we had to count the number of aerials on roofs. If there was more than one then the house was likely to get raided, because the army felt that each household only really needed one, so any others were probably radio aerials for illegal activities. There was also the milk patrol. These were morning patrols in which we would arrange to go down particular streets just after the milkman had completed his rounds. The aim was to count how many bottles he was delivering to each house. The following week we would return with the questionnaire. If, for instance, someone said they lived alone, yet we knew the milkman was delivering six pints of milk, then we might have discovered an IRA safe-house. Of course, the occupant might just have been a fanatical milk drinker, but the place would have got raided all the same. There was no end to the bizarre information they ordered us to collect (number of dogs in street, positioning of lamp-posts and so on). Most of the time they didn't tell us why they needed it – and ours was not to reason why.

The war is fought largely in your own mind and to survive you have to conquer the sinister power of your own imagination, the insidious enemy within. Our foe was invisible. He wore no uniform and held no territory we could attack. To me he was everywhere, looking at me down the barrel of his rifle. The thought of being viewed through the telescopic sights of a sniper's rifle used to unsettle everyone. It was never far from your mind when you were out on patrol. This intense fear of snipers had been fostered in training when our trainers had drummed into us that at some point during a tour we would all come into a sniper's field of vision.

"Bullets travel faster than sound," we used to say to each other, "So you'll never know anything about it." This was comforting only if you assumed the bullet would kill you outright. I assumed it would leave me crippled. So we tried all the time to look for ways of minimising the sniper's chances of getting in a good shot.

Apart from the standard textbook procedures for making yourself a difficult target – zig-zagging, constant movement, keeping heads below parapets – we developed a technique of our own, one that I doubt can be found in any official British Army manual. On republican housing estates we would hand out sweets to children knowing that as they eagerly swarmed around us they'd effectively be shielding us. No IRA sniper would dare fire at a soldier surrounded by children, especially Catholic children. Obviously, neither the children nor their parents knew what we were doing. The idea of using children as sniper-deterrents developed gradually. When we patrolled republican housing estates groups of children would usually follow us, sometimes catcalling and spitting. However, we soon discovered that their apparent loathing for us did not extend to our sweets. At first, we started using the children only when we wanted a quick break. We would crouch down in a doorway and offer any nearby children the Mars bars that usually came with our rations. But some soldiers didn't like handing over their Mars bars. Either they liked eating the bars themselves or they resented giving such a generous present to little Fenians who only moments before might have been abusing them. So we started buying sweets especially to give to the children.

We did it almost as a joke at first, but after a while we became quite serious about it: we would buy lots of the cheap supermarket-own-brand variety which we'd store in our gas-mask holders. Our sweet technique became more sophisticated as time passed – to the extent that we could usually keep children by our side for the whole of our yomp through the estate. They chomped happily, we yomped happily. Sweets soon became as important to us as our flak jackets. Sometimes on patrol you could just have a sixth sense about impending danger. You might have been mistaken – most of the time you probably were – but it was always best to follow those instincts; and at those times when, for whatever reason, a street or a place just didn't feel right we would stop and wait for children to come along.

"Anyone want some sweeties?"

Within seconds they would be swarming around us squealing, "Gimme one! Gimme one!" and we could sweep through the area feeling a lot safer.

We didn't feel we were putting the children at risk, although most of us didn't really care if we were. We used to joke: "If they're old enough to give abuse, they're old enough to take a bullet." No-one could have blamed us if a kid got shot: we wouldn't have pulled the trigger. In a way we were only adapting the army's long-standing practice of building military installations next to schools. Many of what we regarded as the most dangerous republican estates were deprived areas. The children probably didn't get much pocket money for sweets, so a little could go a long way. Over time we became less generous with our hand-outs: we found we could pass through a whole estate with a protective shield of infants secured at little more than the cost of a packet of Opal Fruits.

On 21 May two hunger strikers died, both after 61 days of fasting: Raymond McCreesh, a 24-year-old IRA man, and 23-year-old Patsy O'Hara, of the smaller republican terrorist group, the Irish National Liberation Army (INLA). I remember someone winning the regimental sweepstake. There was particular satisfaction that McCreesh had gone, because he was from the area where the five soldiers had been blown up earlier in the week. He also had a brother who was a priest, which seemed to convince some of the UDR soldiers that God was indeed on their side – not that they'd ever doubted it. Four hunger strikers had now died. No-one now thought that republicans might be bluffing. Now many of us were convinced they'd be willing to lose at least another 20, especially with the worldwide attention they were getting. In Catholic areas we experienced a real groundswell of anti-British hatred. You could really feel the resentment whenever you went out on patrol. Everyone tried to put on the we-don't-care, let's-hope-they-all-fucking-die attitude, but we were all worried.

We transferred a lot of our anxiety into caring for our weapons. Much spare time was taken up sitting on our beds taking our rifles apart, cleaning them, oiling them, checking their every moving part. The thought of a weapon jamming during a "contact" was frightening enough to make even me extremely conscientious in that area at least. However, my shooting skills remained dire and I tended to doubt whether I would be much use in a firefight anyway, unless the enemy was very close. We were given regular target practice at St Angelo, partly to ensure our sights were set correctly. We had to sit in shooting tunnels – concrete pipes, in fact – at the end of which sat the targets. We would shoot off a few rounds and the instructors would bring up the targets for inspection. They would establish whether you were shooting too much to the right or to the left. If necessary, they would adjust your sights by tweaking them with a special little tool. The adjustment was meant to ensure that when you fired you at least hit the target in its central area, if not always in the bull's-eye. I frequently missed the target completely – with or without adjustment. This used to puzzle the instructors: "You're inside the tunnel, you cunt. You can't miss." They could not adjust my sights if they did not know where I was shooting. I think some of them thought I was playing games. I wish I had been.

The deaths of the two hunger strikers on the same day brought a whirlwind of violence across Northern Ireland. Around 10,000 petrol bombs were thrown at the security forces in the week that followed. Fortunately, none of them was aimed at me. On patrol we encountered a lot of hostility, but it was more often of the brooding, silent kind, which in some ways was more difficult to deal with. The camp was always buzzing with activity. As St Angelo was the main headquarters for Fermanagh there were all sorts of people drifting in and out, including lots of spooks (members of military intelligence) or people I assumed were spooks. You never knew for sure: they never spoke to anyone. The SAS team also kept themselves to themselves. There were several SAS men – and you wouldn't even get a hello out of them. A lot of keep-fit lunatics used to run around the camp with bricks or other weights strapped to their legs or backs. One of the SAS men trumped the lot by sticking a huge tractor tyre on his back, attached by ropes, and running around at all hours. Perhaps he was hoping to attract snipers.

In the week of the funerals of McCreesh and O'Hara the Reverend Ian Paisley boosted morale in the television room when he suggested on camera that shotguns ought to be issued to soldiers for use against street rioters. After the terrible onslaught of 10,000 petrol-bombs he thought that shot-guns would be able to clear streets of rioters without risking life in the way a bullet from a rifle might. The packed TV room burst into laughter and cheers. Some people stood on chairs and made Nazi salutes, chanting "Sieg Heil! Sieg Heil!" His idea certainly had popular appeal among soldiers, although we felt the human-rights people might not approve. Another unorthodox weapon that was talked about among squaddies around this time was the PP9-size battery. We had heard that some squaddies were putting these batteries down the barrels of plastic-bullet guns to be fired at rioters along with the plastic bullets. Paisley got another cheer when he mentioned Fermanagh and South Tyrone. Apparently someone had suggested handing the constituency over to the Irish Republic.

The Reverend said: "I would not be prepared to allow any part of my country to leave the United Kingdom."

More cheering, Nazi salutes and shouts of: "Not an inch! Not an inch!"

But outside the TV room there was less bravado. People were tense and on edge, always expecting the worst, especially outside the camp. Normally in a Portakabin full of 20 soldiers you would expect a lot of horse-play and larking around, but people were too wound up to have any fun. I tried playing a few practical jokes, but they always backfired, especially if they involved objects dropping from the sky or sudden loud bangs. People were just too fragile. I would usually end up being screamed at hysterically by someone who in Germany might have laughed off my antics. Then at night it wasn't unusual to hear someone crying. I thought it wimpish, but I'd ignore it so long as the person was merely sobbing quietly into his pillow. I would only say something if thundering sobs disturbed my sleep. Then I would sometimes shout, "Shut up, you wimp," although other soldiers in the room usually shouted me down: "Leave him alone! Leave him alone!" What used to make me really sick was that the ones who soaked their pillows with tears were often the ones writing the war-hero letters to their dopey girlfriends. People often used to leave half-written letters lying around, so, being interested in the literary styles of military men, I'd read them. Some were unbelievable. They would leave me thinking, "This person is not in the same war I'm in. He's in Vietnam."

We had one spectacular crack-up. My brick of four was on foot patrol in a small village. Two of us were on one side of the street, two on the other. Suddenly the soldier in front of me sunk to his knees, letting his rifle clatter on the ground. Then he burst into tears. He just knelt there sobbing at the side of the road. Everyone panicked. We couldn't run to him, because we would have presented too easy a target to any waiting terrorists. But we could hardly leave him there, sobbing in the street for all to see. There were a few civilians around and, although they seemed politely to ignore what was going on, we didn't want to leave them with the image of a soldier whimpering in the gutter.

I kept shouting at him: "Get up, you cunt!" But he kept crying. We got on the radio and got people to come out and pick him up. Fortunately it was a quiet area and we weren't too far away from a base, so a Land Rover arrived very quickly and he was thrown into the back like a piece of rubbish. The man had had a complete breakdown. I was extremely angry with him. If he had felt that bad he shouldn't have left the camp. In a different situation he could have got us all killed. We heard later that it wasn't even the stress of Ireland that had got to him. Apparently he had just found out that his wife in Germany was being unfaithful to him. And worse – she was starring in porno movies in Hamburg.

He was transferred rapidly out of Northern Ireland. I never saw him again.

15

Pray for His Holiness

I HAD been separated from my two best friends when we had first arrived in Northern Ireland – and I didn't see them again until we were back in Germany.

I found myself at St Angelo with people I hardly knew and, although I got on well with a few of them, I kept most of them at a distance. Things weren't helped by the fact that I seemed to be with different people every time I went on patrol. The only constant figure in my life from the old days was the officer we had nicknamed Major Disaster or MD. My usual problems with figures of authority didn't manifest themselves with him, probably because in my eyes he didn't have any authority. I knew he was as reluctant a soldier as I was. That knowledge gave us a shared bond. He was there to keep his daddy happy and I was there to keep out of prison. I had a good relationship with him and at times I felt we had a true friendship. Often on VCPs we would sit talking into the small hours about our very different lives and upbringings.

MD conformed and always had – it made financial sense – whereas I had always rebelled. I think he liked what he saw as my free spirit and he would treat my antics with amused horror. Instead of ticking me off he would laugh and say: "Please, O'Mahoney. Not in front of me, you uncouth bastard." He was a strangely innocent character, vulnerable even. He could not spot danger and did not wish ill on anybody. I tended to see danger everywhere and wished ill on everybody. So although I liked him personally, I didn't particularly enjoy going on patrol with him, because he was always doing things that jarred the nerves. In the countryside dairy farmers would leave milk destined for the creamery in churns on wooden platforms by the sides of roads. The IRA had often used these milk-churns as bombs and most of us were extremely wary of them. In fact when you saw one your first thought was: "Bomb" – a good example of how the fear of terrorism distorts your imagination. You're scared of everything; you're scared of what might be there, even though most of the time it's not there. There were procedures for dealing with milk churns which usually meant taking a detour around them. MD's technique was to walk right up to them, take off the lid and stick his head inside. We would scurry for cover whenever we saw him striding off amiably down the road towards a milk-churn. He wasn't fearless, just clueless.

He was always in trouble, because of the mess he made of everything. In the best comic traditions of the well-meaning British amateur he would bumble into complicated situations

– and make them worse. Some of our patrols had a truly pantomime quality. While our pantomime performances were normally only witnessed by a few civilians, there were a few occasions when a senior officer got a ringside seat. One time a colonel decided to join us on a countryside patrol. He should never have come out with us, because he was too much of a target, but I suppose he'd wanted to make the point that he wasn't just a pen-pusher, that he could hack his way through hedgerows with the lads.

MD had said to us before the colonel joined us at the briefing: "Let's put on a good show. Everything by the book." We tried not to let MD down. A helicopter dropped us in the middle of nowhere. We moved across open ground following the textbook procedure with MD leading from the front, desperately trying to remember everything he had been taught at Sandhurst. It was really a process of running and hiding behind rocks and hedges. At any one time half of you are covering the half who are on the move. So you would zig-zag for 15 to 20 yards, drop to the ground, preferably behind a rock or a hedge, and point your rifle at the cows. Then at the patrol leader's signal the other half would zig-zag past you to a point in front and do the same. The patrol leader needs to co-ordinate this movement efficiently to make sure no-one is left behind. Unfortunately, after we had travelled across several fields of peat-bog MD realised he had left the colonel behind: he was still crouched behind a hedge two fields back waiting for the order to advance. I only realised what had happened when MD, flushed and sweating, stood up and told us we were going back the way we had come. We retraced our steps until we reached the colonel whose rage-filled face peeped out from behind the hedge where he'd been left. He didn't say anything to Major Disaster in front of us, but MD told me later that back at camp the colonel had given him "a few words of advice".

None of us liked having senior officers accompanying us on patrol. Fortunately, they didn't feel the need to put their lives on the line too often. We had been told from the first day in Northern Ireland that outside camp in front of civilians we were never to address officers as "Sir". And they would never wear badges of rank. These precautions were meant to prevent terrorists identifying them as officers (although I'd have thought that in most cases, especially in our "cavalry" regiment, officers only had to open their well-spoken mouths to be identified as officers). The thinking was that an officer would present a more tempting target than a mere squaddie. I understood the logic of this, but I still resented it, especially when the officers who in camp would put you on a charge for not calling them "Sir" were the ones who outside camp would be most upset if you called them "Sir". At checkpoints I made a point of calling officers "Sir" whenever I could, especially in front of Catholics.

Some officers would get really freaked: "O'Mahoney! Don't call me 'Sir'. How many times do you have to be told?"

There was one senior officer I especially loathed: rosy cheeks, little round glasses and a squeaky voice. He looked like that runt out of the *Carry On* films. One day Major Disaster informed us that this officer was going to come out with us. I thought: "Another idiot to carry." We spent the day setting up roving checkpoints. You were supposed to be polite to civilians ("Good evening, Madam. Could I see your driving licence, please? Thank you."), although that was not something I usually managed. However, whenever the senior officer was in earshot I tried to be reasonably civil. We set up a checkpoint in an area which contained a few notorious republican families. We would carry a green field book containing cards with pictures and details of known and suspected terrorists.

In that area there was one family that seemed to take up a whole volume. One branch ran a pub. The husband had gone on the run in the Republic, but his wife had stayed behind to be unpleasant to soldiers. She would torch you with her hatred and abuse. I'd encountered her a few times and come close to breaking my vow never to hit a woman. I was sure we were going to bump into her: she was the type who'd drive around all day and night in the hope of meeting soldiers to abuse. She didn't disappoint me: just as the sun was going down she drove into view. I made her stop the car. Major Disaster and the other officer were standing nearby, but at the passenger side. This meant they could hear only what I said, not what she said. With this in mind I asked her for her licence politely.

She replied: "You fucking English bastard." I think two soldiers or policemen had been killed in Belfast earlier in the day. She added that I would burn in hell with those bastards.

I dropped the mask of politeness and started swearing at her loudly, telling her to give me the fucking licence or I would drag her out of the car and take it off her. I could see the senior officer's face changing to a look of deep concern. He was clearly horrified to hear me talking in this way to a woman.

I heard him say to MD: "I think I'd better deal with this."

MD said to me: "Mahoney, move."

The senior officer came round to the driver's side and said: "I'm very sorry about this, madam. May I see your driving licence?"

She stared at him for about a second, before shouting: "You

fucking four-eyed English bastard. I hope you burn in fucking hell with . . ." I doubt whether he had heard a woman swear before, let alone swear at him. He wouldn't have looked more shocked if she had pulled out a gun and shot him. He stepped back and told me to deal with it.

I pulled open her door and stuck my head right in so that I was inches from her face. I told her to give me the licence or she was coming out of the car by her hair. She handed me the licence.

When she had driven off the officer said: "Top marks, O'Mahoney. That's how to deal with them."

I said: "Thank you, Sir." He said: "Don't call me 'Sir' out here. You should know that by now."

Back at St Angelo someone put up on the noticeboard a leaflet issued by the well-known Catholic priest, Fr Denis Faul. It contained advice about the legal rights of those detained by the security forces. It included one line which caused great amusement: "Suffer patiently while they beat you up." The funniest bit, however, was the section on what soldiers could and could not do at checkpoints. The leaflet read:

1. Give your name, address, where you are coming from and going to.

2. Do not answer any other questions about age, occupation or religion.

3. Do not answer questions about other people, your family, relatives or neighbours.

4. The security forces cannot photograph you against your will.

5. When your car is being searched lock it and say "Which part do you wish to search first?" Accompany the uniformed man and unlock the

boot, then lock it, unlock the car and bonnet in turn, locking each section in turn.

6. If you dislike the way you are being treated (and especially any attempt by men to search women) you have the right to be searched in the nearest RUC station.

7. They are not allowed to take any person away from the well-lit area of the public road – to take persons up side-roads or into fields or up the road on their own is a crime, as it is threatening behaviour.

8. Any undue delay is illegal.

9. Report to me or to your solicitor any grievance you have about fear being inflicted on you or your family on the public road by abuses of Emergency powers.

There was only one thing on that list that I hadn't done to civilians at checkpoints – take photographs. For a while the injunction "suffer patiently" became a sort of comedian's catchphrase around the camp. If anything went wrong for you someone was bound to tell you to "suffer patiently". And when we swapped stories in the canteen about hostile encounters with the locals we would use the term as a euphemism for violence: "Did you make him suffer patiently?" "Yes, he suffered very patiently."

There were always opportunities for violence, but the presence of officers or older and wiser NCOs meant that, a lot of the time, I behaved better than I might otherwise have done. Hunger strikers dwindling slowly towards their end made sure there was always tension in the air. Everything seemed to be going the Provos' way: in the Irish Republic two hunger strikers got elected to parliament in the June general election – and on the same day eight IRA men awaiting sentence for the murder of an SAS soldier escaped from custody in Belfast.

I had only ever known Northern Ireland during the Hunger Strike, so I knew no different. But soldiers who had been born in the area, and UDR and RUC people, all said that things had got much worse. There was a lot more defiance and aggression from Catholics, especially young Catholic men, who tended to be the sort of people we got into scrapes with at checkpoints. It seemed at times that every young nationalist wanted to do his bit for the hunger strikers by getting stroppy with soldiers. Perhaps they saw getting a beating from us as a rite of passage. I could understand them. I knew I would have been the same. It is difficult to describe how I felt. It was not exactly a case of being torn between two sides – I knew which side I was on. I was a British soldier and I had no time for the IRA, and yet I secretly admired the hunger strikers, even though sometimes I could feel elated at their deaths. The strange thing was that while I could allow myself to feel satisfied that a hunger striker had died, I didn't like to see English soldiers, especially middle-class officers, sneering at hunger strikers' deaths. Contradiction was the dominant force within my mind.

I admired the way that even before a hunger striker was buried his successor had been named. Anyone could see they were not isolated fanatics: there were people queueing up to give their lives for the cause. Their resolve impressed me and underlined the fact that we were in a war we could not win, at least not at a price anyone was willing to pay. Some days I would feel a traitor to my uniform for thinking like this, especially when I'd read of the latest IRA atrocity and the pompous statement of justification that usually went with it.

Everyone was so self-righteous; no-one was wrong. We all made our own excuses for our own acts of brutality. Life was full of injustice: everyone behaving unjustly to everyone else. That was the way of the world, it seemed to me. I had felt this from an early age and, in some ways, I suppose this feeling helped me resolve the contradictions I experienced in my mind. I stopped getting bothered about who was right and who was wrong. Everyone was right and everyone was wrong. My only goal was survival.

I was manning a permanent VCP near the border one evening. I was in the central part, checking driving licences. A man in his early forties drove towards me. Word came through on my radio that the driver was a "blue devil" – an IRA sympathiser and low-level helper, the sort of person who would pass on information rather than pull a trigger or plant a bomb himself. I thought: "You sneaky fucker." He stopped and wound down his window. I told him I wanted to search his car.

He said: "I'm only after being searched."

I said I didn't care: I wanted to search him again. I could tell he was in a hurry, which pleased me. With the help of another soldier I started taking everything out of his car, slowly, and checking everything and everywhere, slowly. I let my colleague continue while I started asking questions of the blue devil.

"Name?"

"What's it got to do with you?"

"Address?"

"What's it got to do with you?"

"Age?"

"What's it got to do with you?"

"Religion?" But before he could answer I said: "Catholic."

At this point my colleague stuck his head out of the disordered car and asked the man to come over.

My colleague pointed at a piece of dirt on the carpet and said: "What's that?"

The man said it looked like dirt. My colleague said: "Dirt? It looks like explosives to me. Get the sample bag, Bernie."

If you came across suspicious substances that you thought needed analysis you were supposed to pick them up with a pair of surgical pliers and place them in a special sample bag. Then you had to get the motorist to sign for the bag.

I asked the blue devil to sign, but he refused: "I'm not signing nothing."

I said: "Fucking sign it." He still refused and started shouting at me. I grabbed him by the lapels of his jacket. Instinctively, he grabbed me back. That was enough: that was assault and I was entitled to defend myself. I headbutted him full in the face. The impact sent him instantly to the floor. He lay there dazed, not unconscious, just not saying anything. I was going to give him a kicking on the floor, but Major Disaster came running over and intervened. He told me to deal with another motorist who had just driven in. I walked away.

Back at St Angelo my relationship with Elizabeth was progressing, just as my relationship with the other UDR soldiers was about to decline to a very low point. I was sitting in the canteen one day with a group of soldiers from my regiment. Someone was reading an Irish newspaper. There were reports about the Pope's convalescence after his shooting in Rome. There was also a double-page pull-out poster showing him in better days celebrating mass in front of a huge crowd. In one hand he held his shepherd's crook; his other hand was raised to give a blessing to the people. Underneath the photo were the words: "Pray for His Holiness".

I had an idea for a wind-up. I knew a joint RUC/UDR patrol was about to come in to the canteen. I got some sticky tape from somewhere and stuck the poster above the hot-plate. I sat back down with my mates and we all started giggling. Around five minutes later a group of about twelve UDR and RUC men walked in as expected. Among them was Billy Bunter, the one who kept calling me a Fenian and telling me to keep my head down in a gun-fight. They made their way towards the hot-plate, talking and laughing. We pretended to eat our food.

Suddenly I heard Billy Bunter shout: "You Fenian bastard!" I looked up and he was pointing at the poster. What happened next was extraordinary: at least six UDR men ran to the poster and tore it violently from its place. Then in a group frenzy they ripped it to pieces, spat on it and finally stamped on it, all the time shouting madly. My mates and I were laughing at their antics. Billy saw us and ran over, his face afire with anger. He looked at me and shouted: "Who put that up there? Who fucking put that up there?"

I said: "What are you talking about, you idiot?" We denied having anything to do with it – and no-one outside my group had seen me put it up.

Billy said: "You saw it up there and you did nothing about it." They were all deadly serious; I'm sure they would have been less offended by a bomb. Elizabeth told me later that two of the UDR people had gone to the ops room to see if anyone knew who had put it up: they actually asked an officer if he would launch an enquiry to find the culprit. Fortunately, he decided there were other more urgent priorities. I told

Elizabeth I'd done it purely as a joke. Even she was a bit po-faced about it, telling me I shouldn't have done it, although she accepted that Billy and his boys had over-reacted a little. The incident created a lot of bad feeling between our regiment and the UDR. It overshadowed the rest of the tour. It seemed to confirm the suspicions of some UDR soldiers that our regiment was a haven for IRA sympathisers.

I couldn't understand the mentality of people like Billy Bunter. I wish I could say he was unusual, but he wasn't. That sort of demented anti-Catholicism was widespread. If I had not been going out with Elizabeth I think I would just have dismissed the UDR soldiers as sectarian bigots, but she made me see more clearly how the activities of republicans helped to form people like Billy. Shortly after that incident in the canteen a part-time UDR man from St Angelo was shot dead by the IRA. His name was Tommy Graham. He had been delivering groceries to a cottage near Lisnaskea. The Provos had taken over the house and held its occupant hostage before Tommy had arrived on his regular run. I'd never met him, but I'd seen him around. Elizabeth knew him well. When she talked about him I realised I had met his wife only a few weeks earlier. We had been on patrol and she had invited us in for a cup of tea. I remembered her telling us she had a husband in the UDR. She had mentioned his brother, another UDR man, who had survived an assassination attempt the previous year when he had been ambushed a few hundred yards from his home. He had been shot in the neck and shoulder, but had survived. On the evening news I recognised soldiers from our regiment standing guard by the house where Tommy had been shot. Elizabeth was very upset. She went to the funeral. He was buried with full military honours near Brookeborough. He was 38 and left behind two children aged 12 and 14.

Not long after his funeral my three days' "Rest and Recuperation" finally came up. It was the middle of June, about midway through our tour. It coincided with the court case that had been hanging over me at home for the riot I had started outside the nightclub on my last leave. I had been charged under the Public Order Act with threatening behaviour. I had informed the army of the court case and they had arranged for an officer to attend to speak on my behalf. I had long stopped worrying about my criminal past catching up on me. As far as I was concerned the army knew about my record – and didn't care. My main fear was that the magistrates would be less forgiving. I knew that with my list of previous convictions I would almost certainly get a custodial sentence if I were a civilian. But I was confident my army service and the fact I was risking my life in Northern Ireland would count in my favour.

I got a lift in the covert car to Aldergrove Airport. I wanted to fly to Birmingham, but I could only get a flight to Heathrow. Once there I got the underground into the heart of London. I remember getting off at Piccadilly and wandering around, almost dazed by the lights and the noise of the traffic. I felt strange and uneasy. Mentally I was still in Northern Ireland and I remember wishing I had my rifle with me. I felt naked and vulnerable without it. I went for a drink in a tourist pub and stayed till closing time. I tried chatting up some tourists, but the conversation didn't flow. I must have appeared a bit odd and edgy. As the alcohol settled into my stomach I began to feel more relaxed. By the end of the evening I just felt huge relief to be away from it all. Only a few hours earlier I had been in the middle of Fermanagh and now I was in

London's West End. I ended up missing my train back to Wolverhampton and had to spend the night in Euston Station.

I got an early train back home. I went straight to the magistrates' court. In the foyer I saw the officer who was going to represent me. I could hardly have missed him – he was dressed in full cavalry regalia. I introduced myself to him. He was tall and distinguished-looking and spoke with a pukka accent. I knew he'd go down well with the magistrates. I had never met him before and didn't recognise him from Northern Ireland. In court the prosecution gave a vivid description of the riot: bricks, bottles, spanners, knives, iron bars, wooden stakes, smashed windows, terrified neighbours, fighting in gardens, shredded rose-bushes. It was not the sort of event that usually happened in Codsall – and the magistrates looked less than happy.

My officer stood up to give me a character reference. He said I was a fine soldier, a vital part of the unit, and I was doing a sterling job in Ulster at a very difficult and dangerous time. He said if I received a custodial sentence I would be expelled from the army, which would be a tragedy as I had a wonderful military career ahead of me. He was very impressive, although I thought he was talking about someone else. I had pleaded guilty, so the magistrates only had to decide my sentence. My previous convictions were read out in the hearing of the officer and then the magistrates left the court to make their decision. I wasn't worried. I thought my officer had probably swung it for me, and I was right. I was given an £80 fine with £20 costs.

Outside the court the officer shook my hand. He said: "Good show, O'Mahoney. You gave those blighters a good hiding."

The local paper, the *Wolverhampton Express and Star*, carried a full report on the court case. It was a page lead with the headline, "Gang fight on car park was open warfare." It read:

> Rival gangs armed with knives, iron bars, spanners and bottles fought a pitched battle on a Wolverhampton pub car park, magistrates were told.
>
> Residents feared for their safety while hysterical youths savagely attacked each other outside the Wheel Inn in Wolverhampton Road, Codsall, said Mr Aidan Cotter, prosecuting, yesterday.
>
> Youths broke bottles in the road and chased each other over gardens.
>
> "What happened was the worst disturbance that has ever been known in Codsall. It amounted to gang warfare," magistrates' chairman, Mr Harold Ambler, told the court yesterday.

I kept my head down for the next few days: I didn't want to push my luck. It was good to see family and friends again, but no-one seemed particularly surprised or even pleased to see me. I suppose I was disappointed by their reaction. I had not expected to be welcomed home as a conquering hero, but at the same time I would have appreciated just a little acknowledgement that I had been risking my life in a dangerous place. Their reactions only confirmed what I knew already: few people in England cared about what went on in Northern Ireland.

16

Hooligans Make the Best Soldiers

I WAS only on special leave for three days, but something surprising happened in that time – I found I was missing Northern Ireland and looking forward to getting back.

Life in Codsall seemed hugely dull. The place looked much the same. The chat was much the same. My friends were doing much the same as they had always done. I found I couldn't relate to them, or civilian life, in the way I used to. Life in the army in Northern Ireland could be dull too, but not in the same way. The backdrop of conflict and the ever-present threat of violence meant that even when things were apparently dull I lived in a state of alertness. The fear and tension made me feel I was at least living life wide-awake. In Codsall everyone seemed half asleep, if not comatose.

On the flight back to Belfast I felt happy in a way I hadn't felt for some time. I was actually looking forward to getting back in uniform and out on patrol. The covert car picked me up at the airport and drove me down to St Angelo. I remembered how petrified I'd been the first time I'd travelled this route. Now, only two months later, I felt relaxed. There was danger out there, but I'd proved to myself I could handle it. I had learnt to control my fear. I was still paranoid and watchful, yet I felt my mind could no longer torture me with its imaginings. In some ways I thought I was in more danger from other soldiers than from the IRA. Since the first few weeks no more soldiers had shot themselves or their mates, but I wasn't sure how long the regiment's good fortune would last. As I had grown more confident in my own soldiering abilities I had grown more contemptuous of others' inabilities.

I didn't mind people like Major Disaster – he made no pretence of being a proper soldier – it was more the army-barmies I used to mock, the ones who could probably have identified by silhouette every type of Soviet attack helicopter and scored only bull's-eyes on the firing range, but who on the ground in Northern Ireland dealing with real people in real situations were frequently clueless. On the other hand people like me and Mac, natural born hooligans, barely capable of identifying one end of a rifle from the other, could deal effectively with any trouble that came our way, even if we caused a lot of it ourselves. In my mind hooligans made the best soldiers.

I started drinking a lot more. There was little else to do when you were not working, apart from watching television.

I remember June for the hours spent watching tennis from Wimbledon. Tennis and news bulletins and home-videos sent by soldiers' wives in Germany. There was sometimes a bit of tension caused by the way married soldiers would casually interrupt programmes as they piled in to watch the latest video nasties from their gormless spouses ("Hello, Pete. Dorothy sends her love. Tabby's had some more kittens. Keep your head down."). Sometimes the bar was the only refuge: I could usually rely on Mac as a drinking partner. Others would tut-tut as we got steamed up in the bar. They would tell us we were mad, that we shouldn't, that in the morning we wouldn't be thinking straight. I used to reply that if someone was going to shoot me I didn't want to be thinking straight. Mac and I even started bringing alcohol with us on night-time checkpoint shifts. The places in our gas-mask holders which by day were filled with sweeties by night were filled with cans of lager. We would also stash cans in our combat jackets. I can't remember us ever being drunk on duty, with our loaded rifles, but four pints of lager mixed with adrenaline probably contributed to our more loutish behaviour at checkpoints. We used to say that at least the booze helped us walk in zig-zags.

I started really enjoying myself on patrol or at checkpoints. I really did get into it. The more confident I got the more enjoyable I found it. There are some people who should never be put in positions of power – and I was certainly one of them. I began to relish the opportunities for confrontation, especially as the people who used to confront us tended to be around my age. I would experience the same buzz I used to get from gang fights and I'd behave in much the same way as I did formerly. The difference was that now I wore a uniform, carried a gun and acted with lawful authority. But, for all that, we very rarely gave anyone a serious beating. If anyone ended up in hospital they would only have arrived there with a wound that could have been patched up quickly in casualty. Most of the time I doubt whether we even inflicted wounds as serious as that. It would just be a punch here, a kick there, the odd headbutt or dig in the ribs with a rifle. And, as far as I was concerned, I never hit anyone who didn't ask for it. If stroppy young men wanted to do their bit for Ireland by testing me I was willing to meet the challenge. So was Mac.

One evening we had been setting up roving checkpoints near the border. We stopped a mini-bus which contained about eight men, aged between 25 to 35, from Monaghan in the Republic, a place we had been led to believe was an IRA stronghold. They were on their way somewhere for a night out and they didn't like us interrupting their drinking time. We ordered them out of the bus and they grudgingly assembled in the road. They complained loudly about the delay as we searched the bus. But then they started swearing, calling us "fucking Brits" and – a favourite local term – "whores". If they had kept their mouths shut we would probably just have searched the bus and sent them on their way. The cheekiest one said: "We won't forget your faces." We started searching them individually. Charisma, the fundamentalist Protestant, was with us. He was about to search the cheekiest who pulled away from him saying, "You're not searching me." He tried to step back onto the bus, but Charisma grabbed him and pulled him back. The young man turned and squared up to him. Charisma stepped back. The man's friends, sensing Charisma's fear, moved forward aggressively. Mac was nearest to the man who had tried to get back on the bus – and smashed the flat of his rifle butt into the side of his head. The victim fell to the floor, temporarily stunned.

In my eyes what Mac did was brutal, but necessary. The situation had been on the verge of getting out of control – and someone could have ended up shot. Instead the men shut their mouths and did as they were told. We finished searching everybody, even the man on the floor who gradually came to, and they all got back on the mini-bus. Of course we knew such incidents bred hatred and helped swell the IRA's ranks, but we didn't care. Our overriding goal was to get back to camp, and ultimately to Germany, alive and intact. The future was someone else's problem.

Friday and Saturday evenings were often the worst for trouble. These were the times when the roads seemed packed with car-loads of young men, often half-drunk, moving back and forth across the border in search of a night out. A favourite destination for people from the north was a so-called country club in the Republic. We had been told it was popular with disco-dancing Provos. We got to know the faces of a lot of the teenagers who would pass through most weekends on their way to the club. Some of them would even try to sell us raffle tickets – with proceeds going to republican prisoners' families.

One Friday night I found myself on a shift at the permanent checkpoint nearest the club. Major Disaster was in charge. Not all of us were on duty: there were four of us grabbing a few hours' sleep. I was snoozing; Mac was snoring. Suddenly another soldier came in and roused us.

He said: "Quick. You're wanted. There's a group of paddies gonna kick off." Apparently one of them had even made to grab Major Disaster's rifle.

I jumped up quite easily, rifle lashed to my arm, but Mac had been sleeping soundly and we had to dig him for a few seconds to bring him to life. He was a huge man, tall and stocky, and he didn't like having his sleep disturbed. It could have been a scene out of a wildlife film where the camera-crew stumbles upon a hungry grizzly bear. He gave a roaring yawn which showed off his missing front teeth. I followed him outside where we could see Major Disaster and a few other soldiers in a stand-off with four over-excited men screaming abuse. Mac didn't say anything: he just walked straight over to the group and punched the first man full in the face. The man fell on the floor and Mac started kicking him viciously. The man's friends were stunned into silence, while he himself squirmed on the ground trying to avoid Mac's boot.

Major Disaster shouted: "Stop it! Stop it! That's enough."

We made them all sit on the ground with their legs crossed. One of them asked if they could smoke. I had an idea. I said they could smoke, but I wanted them to move further down the road to do so. We were surrounded by hills. I made them sit in the road at the darkest and most exposed point in the VCP. They looked a bit nervous. One of them asked why we were making them sit there. I pointed to the hills and said that if there was a sniper up there hoping to shoot a soldier all he would see were the lights of the cigarettes. They jumped to their feet and stamped out their cigarettes, shouting: "You're trying to get us killed!" We let them go eventually. The next time they passed through they were a lot less cocky.

Our favourite game of harassment was also the simplest – delaying people at checkpoints, especially when you knew they were in a hurry. You could do a quick search or a slow search or, for the area's Owen Carrons, a very slow search. And then you could radio ahead to a patrol up the road and they could repeat the procedure. If you were in the patrol up ahead, you wouldn't usually know why you were being asked to stop people for a second time. You didn't need to know. If your mates were telling you to stop them then they had to be bad bastards and that was that. You treated them accordingly, no matter how respectable they looked.

I remember being on a roving patrol when we got a call on the radio telling us to stop a car that was coming our way and which had just been searched. It was a country road and we had been hiding in bushes. The car came towards us and I jumped into the road, put my hand up and shouted: "STOP!" Inside the car were four people, all dressed for ballroom dancing. On the back seat were a middle-aged couple: she was wearing a long, black ballgown, he was in a dinner jacket. In the front passenger seat was an old man, smartly dressed but very frail. He looked like he had a week to live. It was raining heavily and they already looked as if they had been dragged through a hedge by the first patrol. The driver wound down his window. His face, streaked with rain drops, flashed with anger and exasperation.

He said: "I've just been stopped."

I said I didn't give a fuck: I wanted to see his driving licence.

He said again: "But I've just been stopped. Up the road."

I said: "How the fuck do we know that? Out of the car." As they got out of the car the woman remonstrated with me angrily. I said: "Oh fucking shut up."

The old man was still in his seat and showed no signs of moving. I said I wanted granddad out as well. They said he was old and infirm. I said I didn't care. They helped the old man out of his seat. He was so frail he had to lean against the bonnet. The rain continued to fall, soaking everyone even more. We started emptying the car. We took out all the mats and unloaded everything from the boot, including the spare wheel. Then we put everything back again, slowly. All the time the woman would not stop complaining. Finally we let them get back into the car.

Then, just as the driver was about to close his door I said to Mac loudly: "Are you sure you checked under the back seat?"

Mac looked at me and twisted his face into a mask of mockingly exaggerated regret: "I don't think I did."

I said to the driver: "Right. Everyone out of the car." And we repeated the procedure, this time pulling out the back seat. When they finally set off I'm sure they headed for the nearest IRA recruitment officer and offered their services. I cringe now when I think of the way we behaved then, but we were in a war and we left any decency back at camp.

Two more IRA hunger strikers died in July: 30-year-old Joe McDonnell was the fifth, after fasting for 61 days; Martin Hurson, aged 27, went after 46 days. There were jokes back at camp that he had deliberately died a lot earlier than the others just to stop any of us winning the sweepstake with an accurate guess. On the Saturday of the week in which he died we watched news reports of a huge riot in Dublin where republicans had tried to storm the British Embassy. Around 200 people had been injured.

It was around this time that Nasty interfered with mourners heading for one of the hunger striker's funerals. I was not there and I never found out exactly what he did, but I heard it was something to do with a hearse. Whatever it was it outraged the mourners who were in several cars. They all got out and there was a scuffle. Soon afterwards we were told in briefings not to interfere in any way with mourners, especially those crossing the border. Everyone had to be waved through without being searched. This annoyed us, because whole coach-loads of people used to cross from the Republic on their way to hunger strikers' funerals. We thought that as soon as they realised they weren't going to be searched they would be filling the coaches with weaponry for their IRA friends in the north. For the rest of the tour we had to stand by while coaches drove past us filled with people holding up tricolours, making rude gestures and mouthing obscenities, their faces contorted with hatred. We assumed the non-intervention order had come about because of all the foreign journalists in the province. The army didn't want foreigners filming us harassing mourners. We might have appeared inhumane.

After the death of a hunger striker local republicans would sometimes hold candlelit vigils outside army bases, usually one of the smaller and more vulnerable bases. I remember one at Rosslea when a crowd sat down in the road blocking the gates so that vehicles couldn't get in or out. They were sitting there with their black flags and candles. I was standing there next to an RUC man. I asked him why the RUC didn't drag them off the Queen's highway.

He looked at me as if I were mad. "It's all right for you," he said, "you'll be gone from here in a few months. I'm going to have to live here."

On patrol near the border you could not always be sure where the border was. At its clearest points there might be a bridge or a river or a sign, but in other places it would be marked only by a hedge or a stream or a white cross in the road. We had strict orders not to cross the border, but we often ignored them, especially in those areas where we could have claimed justifiably that we'd been lost or confused. Usually we did it as a dare when we knew we were being watched by citizens of the Republic. There might be a house with a large garden that we knew was in the Republic. We would cross into the garden and hang around for half an hour, stamping on rose bushes. The house's occupants would stare at us fearfully from the window, but they never came out to point out our error. Sensibly, they stayed where they were. They probably thought we were an SAS death squad. Some of them must have phoned the Irish police to complain, because sometimes back at camp we would be asked if we had crossed the border in such and such an area.

"No, Sir. Not to our knowledge."

However, our worst mischief was reserved for houses on the British side of the border. In the camp's ops room there used to be a board on which were listed the addresses of isolated houses whose occupants were away for whatever reason. The RUC used to encourage people to inform them if their houses were going to be empty for any long periods of time, so the security forces could keep an eye on them. Everyone benefited, supposedly: the owners could holiday happily knowing their houses were safe and we could be alert to those properties terrorists might use as vantage points for attacks.

So before going out on patrol we would often check the board to see whose house was empty. Then we would go there and break in, usually by forcing the back window. We could only do this if officers weren't around and the patrol was being led by a corporal. The purpose was not to steal stuff, although we did occasionally pinch small items; it was really to have a place where we could put our feet up for a few hours and watch TV, instead of footslogging through the countryside. If there was any beer or food around, so much the better, but we'd be happy just to find a comfortable sitting room where we could lounge on the sofa monitoring daytime television. We would usually rummage through the other rooms to see what was there, but we wouldn't cause any damage. And most of the time there wasn't anything worth stealing anyway. If the owners had any money they didn't seem to spend it on possessions.

There was one house in a nature reserve where we found fishing paraphernalia in the shed. We took it out and went down to the nearby river where we spent the day fishing. A few of us kept watch, but we had the river to ourselves. Someone even caught a trout. When it was time to go we put the fishing rods back where we found them. I remember another house where in the hallway there was a hat-stand covered with hats. We all put on various hats and sat in the front room watching TV, laughing and joking whilst doing impersonations of various people.

One time we almost got caught. We had forced the back window of an isolated bungalow. We wandered through the bedrooms. I found myself in what seemed to be a teenage girl's bedroom – posters of pretty-boy pop stars, furry toys, and chocolate wrappers in the bin. She had a cassette player and a small collection of pop tapes. I decided it was time to get a replacement for the Phil Collins tape that had been playing non-stop in our sleeping quarters for almost two months. Unfortunately, almost all her cassettes were home-made, songs taped from Radio One's *Top 40* programme. There was only one professionally-produced album by Rickie Lee Jones who had had a hit called "Chuck E's in Love". I wouldn't have bought it myself, but I felt I could have tolerated anything that replaced the Phil Collins tape. I pocketed the tape.

Other soldiers had settled down in front of the television. I went into the kitchen and opened the fridge. There was a huge, untouched cooked salmon on a plate. I took a chunk out of it and brought it into the sitting room to share with the others. But before they could get their teeth into it we heard the sound of a car's tyres on the gravel driveway outside.

Everyone jumped up. I said: "Out the back!" Someone turned off the TV and we ran out the way we came. I put the salmon back in the fridge. A middle-aged couple and their teenage daughter came around the back to find us wandering round the garden, pretending to check the place out. We must have given a good impression of soldiers doing their duty, because they were really pleased to see us. They even invited us in for a cup of tea. We declined politely. I was closest to the back door and, looking in, I could see our boot marks all over the kitchen's tiled floor.

Then, to my horror, the mother said: "Well, if you won't have a cup of tea, would you like a salmon sandwich, lads?"

I didn't want her to open the fridge in our presence. "No, no, no," I said. "We've just had our rations. We've got to get off."

No-one ever complained about these break-ins, probably because no-one ever thought it was us. Even if the owners had caught us in their house we could easily have explained ourselves. We were the law. And most of them wouldn't have minded anyway: Protestants in rural areas used to glow with delight when they saw us. In urban areas Protestant teenagers used frequently to sit near checkpoints identifying Catholics for us: "He's up to this. He's up to that." Quite blatant they were. My main regret was stealing the Rickie Lee Jones tape. It ended up being played all the time in our Portakabin and I grew to hate it even more than the Phil Collins.

I've spoken to other soldiers who've served in Northern Ireland, especially in Belfast. Several told me how they used to get on the radio to make bogus reports of suspicious packages in shops. They would clear all the shops in a street so the "package" could be checked out. Then they would go into the shops and steal what they wanted.

In the last month of the tour I found myself on a patrol that came under rifle fire. We were moving through lush countryside on one of those rare sun-filled days when Fermanagh could seem like the most beautiful place in the world. We could see no-one. I felt we were out of place, like blots on the landscape, particularly as Nasty was with us. We crossed a field and moved onto a road skirted by a raised hedge. Suddenly – PHEWW! PHEWW! PHEWW! – bullets came tearing through the hedge just above our heads. Everyone dived to the ground.

I flattened myself into the grass verge and held the rifle to my shoulder, ready for firing. I had a special sight on my rifle which improved my vision no end. I looked around. Everyone's eyes were wide with fear. The radio operator was shouting down the line to base: "CONTACT! CONTACT! CONTACT!" Fortunately, we were being led by a corporal I rated highly. A few more bullets came through the hedge and then silence.

The corporal took the initiative. He said we were on low ground and had to get onto high ground to outflank the sniper. The hedge was easier to get through further down the road. The corporal shouted: "Go! Go! Go!"

I think there's a key point in moments of danger when you must force yourself to act, almost without thinking, otherwise fear will paralyse you. A Welsh soldier near me got up and started running. I got up on wobbly legs and followed him. The others were more hesitant: Nasty in particular wasn't moving. He seemed rooted to the spot in shock. So much for his wanting to get at the Fenians. The Welsh soldier and I passed through the hedge and ran straight up the hill from which the shots must have come. I half expected a bullet to crash into me, but the adrenaline had taken over now. The corporal was behind us. I had heard him shouting orders at the others, who had started to emerge from behind the hedge.

The three of us got to the top of the hill. We looked down and there in front of us, quite a distance away but clearly visible, were two male figures, both running, one of them carrying a rifle. We pointed our rifles at them.

Through my special sight I could see as clearly as anything. The sight was an image intensifier, battery operated, and it made a little whining noise as you turned it on. It was designed mainly for night use when you could look through the green haze and pick out heat-sensitive objects. People would come up as shadows. The word was that you could make men sterile by pointing it at their privates, but that was probably a myth. Sometimes at checkpoints we would sit there pointing it at the genitals of motorists who were being searched. Now for the first time I was pointing it at two terrorists who had just opened fire on us.

Even though I was a bad shot I felt I couldn't miss at that range and with that sight. But in that second when I took in the whole scene there was one slight detail that made me think,

"This isn't right." It was a dog: there was a dog running beside the two figures.

The corporal started shouting: "Halt or I fire! Halt or I fire!" But the figures kept running.

I was disappointed he didn't fire. I felt I couldn't pull the trigger until he had. The others from the patrol were now quite a few yards behind us. The corporal shouted back to the radio operator to tell base we'd spotted two suspects. The helicopter carrying the Quick Reaction Force would already have been in the air. The news that there were two running targets would have created great excitement: everyone would have been geared up for a fox hunt. The RUC would probably have been begging to get involved on the ground. We ran after the two figures. I badly wanted to shoot, but I knew something was wrong. The black-and-white collie dog made me know in my heart we were not dealing with terrorists.

I couldn't help myself, though: I still wanted to shoot them. I kept shouting to the corporal: "I can see them. I can see them."

He kept shouting back: "Don't shoot! Don't shoot!"

We must have chased them across three fields. They were clear targets all the time. My urge to shoot almost overwhelmed me and I resented the corporal's caution. He kept telling us to keep following them and not to shoot. As I got to the top of another hillock and watched the two figures running towards a farm I looked through my sight again. I felt real yearning as my finger tensed on the trigger. A little squeeze and they would have been gone.

Within seconds I had lost the opportunity: the figures disappeared into the farm, which consisted of a house, a barn and a small shed. By now the helicopter was hovering above us.

The corporal was on the radio. I heard him say we were going to go into the farmyard. The rest of the patrol had caught up with us. We moved in zig-zags into the farmyard, covering each other. There was a car outside the house. On the back seat was the dog: it was panting madly and its coat was wet.

We kicked open the back door of the house and there, sitting in the kitchen, were two boys, no older than 15. I asked them if they had seen anyone run through the farm. They said they hadn't. "Don't fucking lie to me," I said. "It was you."

The slightly older one said no, but his mate started crying.

I said again: "It was you."

But the older one said: "No, no, no. It wasn't me."

I asked him whether the dog in the car was his. He said it was. I said: "Well, why's your fucking dog panting? It's you, you cunt." He looked down at the ground and said yes.

His mate, who was still crying, said: "What are you after us for?"

They told us what had happened. They were brothers. Their mother was dead and they lived alone with their father, who had gone into town to get some false teeth fitted. They knew he was going to be away for a while, so they had taken out his legally-held rifle and gone into the fields for some target practice. They said they had never seen soldiers in that area and they hadn't seen us until we had started chasing them. When the older one had finished talking I slapped him across the face with the back of my hand. It was a mixture of relief and anger, like the way a mother hits her child when he turns up after she's been worried about him.

"You stupid little cunt," I said, "I could have fucking shot you." The police arrived and we left.

In the following days I felt sick with myself. Even today I

find myself sweating when I think of what almost happened. That incident disturbed me more than anything else I did in Northern Ireland, perhaps more than anything else I've done in my life. Why? Because I felt I had met full-on a real badness within myself. I had desperately wanted to kill those boys. I had known instinctively as soon as I had seen them properly that they were not terrorists. We all had: that was why the corporal kept telling us not to shoot. Yet I had wanted to kill them. I had wanted to pull that trigger and blow them away; and I'd wanted to do it not because they were Irish but because I knew I could have got away with it. Under the army's rules of engagement I knew I could have shot both boys dead with no recriminations. We had come under fire and, after shouting a warning to two armed fugitives who refused to stop, we had returned fire. It would have been a tragic misadventure. The only glimmer of comfort I got from encountering my own darkness was the knowledge that I wouldn't have been able to live with myself if I'd done what I'd wanted to do.

That experience knocked out of me a lot of my new-found soldierly cockiness. It made me feel strange inside. I felt at times as if the badness within me would bring badness upon me. I wondered seriously if I would get out of Northern Ireland alive, even though we had entered the last three weeks of the tour.

On 1 August another hunger striker died, 25-year-old INLA member Kevin Lynch, after 71 days. The next day an IRA hunger striker died, also aged 25. Kieran Doherty had fasted for 73 days and during that time had been elected to the Irish parliament.

Throughout the tour I had been travelling regularly in the covert car to the military dental centre in Omagh where I was being fitted with two new front teeth to replace the originals that had been knocked out at a nightclub. On the day Doherty died the IRA blew up an unmarked police car just outside Omagh, killing two policemen. On the same day in Belfast the IRA fired a rocket at an army Land Rover. A 21-year-old soldier had to have both legs amputated below the knee. I remember watching the news and thinking, "21 – my age – and a cripple." Over the next few days there were concentrated car-bomb and incendiary attacks all over the north and at the end of the week the ninth hunger striker died, 23-year-old IRA man Thomas McElwee. Over that weekend more than 1,000 petrol bombs were thrown at the security forces. The whole place seemed about to go up in flames. My feelings of guilt diminished, my hatred for the terrorists returned. I was soon back to my old self.

With less than two weeks to go everyone was nervous. We had often been told we were most likely to be hit either in the first few weeks when we were "green" or in the last few weeks when we were preoccupied with thoughts of home. The fields around permanent checkpoints became at night a real danger zone for animals. They would walk into the trip wires, setting off flares. At other times they might have escaped with their lives, but we were all so jumpy that if a flare went off we tended to open fire. I only ever saw sheep shot, but others had tales of foxes, rabbits and even the odd cow, being slaughtered. When a flare went off someone had to go out into the darkness amongst the bushes and re-set it. This often led to arguments.

"It's your turn."

"No, it's not. It's yours."

"Fuck off. I'm not going."

One night I was off-duty and sleeping at a permanent

checkpoint. Mac was there. There was no electricity or running water. We used to use paraffin-fuelled storm-lamps for light. They looked like those old miners' lanterns. You had to put the fuel in, pump a small handle and light the wick. So long as the air pressure was kept up by pumping the handle they gave off light. While we were sleeping another soldier filled the lamp and began pumping madly. Suddenly it exploded, bursting into a ball of flame. We found out later that he had filled it with petrol by mistake. His lower leg caught fire and he began screaming as his lightweight green nylon combat trousers melted onto his leg. He threw himself to the ground and began rolling around and kicking his legs and arms, screaming for help. Mac and I jumped up, saw the flames and assumed we'd been petrol-bombed. I ran to hold our mate to stop him moving around in case he set something else on fire, and Mac grabbed a huge water pot which we used to heat water for washing. The soldier was still screaming as Mac ran over and threw the contents of the pot over his leg.

The soldier's screams intensified, "ARGH! ARGH! ARGH!" and he was obviously in greater pain.

Mac looked at the pot and said: "Shit. That was boiling water."

Our friend was whisked off to hospital. Later we got word that the burns to his legs from the boiling water were far more serious than those caused by the petrol.

In those last weeks we kept up our harassment of the prospective MP Owen Carron. The by-election was due to be held on 20 August, the day before our tour ended. On that last night I didn't stay up to hear the election result, but I woke the next day to discover our regiment had obviously failed to win the hearts and minds of the people of Fermanagh-South

Tyrone. The electors had voted overwhelmingly for Owen Carron. The most harassed man in the constituency had won by 2,230 votes. More than 31,000 had elected him to serve as their Member of Parliament. He had got even more votes than the previous MP, the dead hunger striker Bobby Sands. In the canteen his victory dampened any celebration there might otherwise have been over the news of the death of the tenth hunger striker, the 23-year-old INLA man, Michael Devine. On the news Mrs Thatcher said she was bitterly disappointed by Carron's win. As I ate my breakfast at St Angelo for the last time I wondered whether our regiment's presence – and I personally – had contributed towards this boost in the republicans' electoral strength.

One of the Enniskillen-born soldiers said: "We should have shot that cunt when we had the chance."

I couldn't see what difference it would have made. Overall, though, his victory didn't undermine our high spirits. It might have underlined the fact that we weren't winning anything, but none of us really cared: we were getting out of there and that was all that mattered. We just had to get through the last day.

Major Disaster gave us our final briefing. He outlined a slick plan of action for the hand-over to our replacement regiment, the Royal Anglians. We would be on a checkpoint near the border when the Royal Anglians arrived by Wessex helicopter. They would disembark and join us in our positions. During this time the Wessex would fly off and circle briefly before returning to take us on board. The Royal Anglians would cover our orderly departure. That last morning on the checkpoint was an agony of waiting. What if the Provos chose this time to launch an attack? I imagined dying as the helicopter came in to land. I think everyone else was thinking the same. We weren't going to feel safe until we were at least on that helicopter on its way to St Angelo. We divided our time between looking at our watches and staring at the sky, waiting for a longed-for sight of that Wessex and the comforting sound of its rotor blades. In the afternoon a code-word came through on the radio that told us the Wessex was ten minutes away. We checked our rucksacks were secure.

Then in the distant sky we spotted the Wessex. We all looked at each other, beaming, as if to say, "It's over. We're getting out of here." Soon we could hear the DUGG-DUGG-DUGG of the rotor blades as the Wessex swept towards us. Just as it touched the ground we all spontaneously jumped to our feet and ran towards it. The Royal Anglians, proper infantrymen, were jumping out, rolling in the grass and taking up firing positions, doing everything by the book. But before the last one of them had jumped out we had got to the Wessex and started jumping in. It was like one of those pitiful scenes from the Vietnam war: desperate refugees making a dash for the last chopper out of Saigon. The slick hand-over had not gone quite to plan. We had caught the helicopter's loader by surprise. He didn't know whether to tell the pilot to take off, because we were half in and half out. While he was deciding we were hurling our gear in and clambering on. The loader just stood there shaking his head. The Wessex lifted into the air. I looked at Major Disaster and smiled. He was almost laughing: he stuck his thumb up at me. Below us we could see the Royal Anglians looking up at us, gobsmacked. It was a great moment.

We still had the journey in the removal van to Aldergrove Airport, but everyone was a lot more relaxed than on the journey down. When we got to the airport we found ourselves in the same hangar as before. But now we were the jubilant soldiers – and we could watch the arrival of our grim-faced replacements.

A few hours later we were in coaches driving through the gates of Imphal Barracks in Osnabrück. We drove into the massive parade square where a waiting band struck up Cliff Richard's "Congratulations". Just behind the band were a crowd of people waiting to welcome us. They were waving and cheering. We felt chuffed.

Then a sergeant opened the coach's door and said: "Married men off the coach. Single men stay where you are."

The married men filed off and ran to the arms of their waiting wives and children. The regimental photographer took pictures of the embraces. Once everyone had gone, including the band and the photographer, the sergeant came back and told us that once we had unloaded the kit from the coach we could go. We got our gear, unloaded the stores and ambled back to our quarters, deflated.

17

A Job Well Done

THE FIRST few weeks back in Germany were a time of drinking and swapping tales from the war zone.

I caught up with my best friends, Paul and Lofty, whom I hadn't seen since April. They had both emerged unscathed and seemed to have spent their time in tranquil backwaters. I also met Edwards, the soldier wounded in the mortar attack. He said he could hardly remember anything about it. He certainly couldn't remember me being there. He hadn't responded to me when I was trying to help him. Of course, I realised I had kept calling him "Clarkey" for some reason, probably shock. "No wonder I didn't answer you," Edwards said. He did not bad-mouth the Irish over what had happened to him, at least not in my hearing. He just talked about the injuries. The main scar was an awful purple-coloured monstrosity. It was in an L-shape, one end of which was on his back, the other on his right side, about 18 inches in length and half an inch in width. He had another unsightly scar across his cheek and jaw. Fortunately, he had been walking beside a blast-wall when the mortars landed. White-hot shrapnel had spun through the air and torn into him. After seeing his injuries I couldn't call him lucky, but it could have been worse: without the blast-wall to cushion the explosion he would have been "fertiliser".

It was good to be back in a relatively relaxed environment with women and children around the place. Something struck me that I had only half noticed before – the way a lot of soldiers spoke to their wives and children as if they were in the army. NCOs were the worst for this: many of them talked to their loved ones as if they were on parade. You could always spot army kids. They were the ones with creases in their shirts – three down the back, two down the front, one down each sleeve – and highly polished football boots.

I rang Elizabeth in Ireland regularly. We had agreed to try to keep the relationship going, despite the distance. We planned to meet up: she was going to come to Germany for a holiday and I was going to spend Christmas in Enniskillen. She kept me informed about what was going on back at St Angelo. I told her we had all received individual certificates from the chairman of Fermanagh District Council thanking us for having served in the area. I read mine out to her:

In Recognition and Appreciation
of service during four and a half months tour of duty by
24516117 Trooper B.P. O'Mahoney (4th Troop)
with the

5th Royal Enniskilling Dragoon Guards
in County Fermanagh, Northern Ireland
from April 1981 till August 1981

It was decorated with the Fermanagh coat of arms and had been personally signed by the council chairman, Councillor Raymond Ferguson. We all thought it was a nice gesture, although the council had misspelt the regiment's name: it should have been "Inniskilling".

On 3 October 1981 the six remaining hunger strikers called off their action. I read that during the period of the Hunger Strike sixty-one people had died in violent incidents. Among them were fifteen policemen, eight soldiers and seven UDR members. The rest were civilians, including seven people (two of them girls of 11 and 14) who died from injuries inflicted by plastic bullets fired by the police and army.

We seemed to spend most of the next few months on exercises. You would no sooner finish one exercise than you would be preparing for the next. For all our fear of imminent death in Northern Ireland I think it was a statistical fact that a soldier was in more danger of dying on exercise in Germany. We had even been told that the army set an "acceptable" death toll before each exercise. If that number was reached, or exceeded, the exercise would be stopped. It didn't surprise me that so many soldiers died, because they really pushed you. Most accidents would happen with people doing stupid things through tiredness – lorries going off the road or helicopters flying into power lines. Quite a few German civilians would die as well: you would get a family driving up the road in a Volkswagen Beetle and they'd smash into a camouflaged tank parked in a lay-by. Working with tanks carried special dangers. You were told always to sleep on top of a tank. In bad weather some soldiers would sleep underneath because there's a two-foot clearance. However, if the tank was on soft ground it would sink gradually over the course of several hours. Then the only way to get it off the person being crushed would be to start the engine and drive off. But sometimes the act of driving off would push the tank down further and any soldiers underneath would be crushed to death. I never saw this happen, but I had heard of it happening a few times when I was in the army.

In the final days of one exercise we were camped in a forest. The weather was bitterly cold and we decided to make a fire using twigs, paper and petrol. As we stood around it talking and warming ourselves a Geordie thought it was not warm enough, so he picked up the bucket containing the petrol, which was about a quarter full, and ineptly threw the remainder towards the fire. The stream of airborne petrol passed through the fire, ignited and continued on its flaming flight towards me. I didn't see it until the last second, when I put my hands up to my face and fell to the floor. I could feel a burning sensation around my right eye and I could hear Paul shouting: "Put him out! Put him out!" Fortunately I was wearing several layers of thick clothing because of the extreme German winter. Paul was beating me, kicking foliage over me and generally causing more damage to me in his efforts to extinguish the flames than would have occurred if he had left me to burn. When I eventually got to my feet, I found I couldn't see properly through my right eye, so I was taken to hospital. They kept me overnight and the next day told me my injury was not serious. Apparently, it had not been caused by the fire, but by the pine needles contained in the foliage Paul had kicked over my face. The fire left me with slight blistering on the face and hands and scorch marks on my clothes.

I kept up my calls to Elizabeth. I liked to hear what was going on at St Angelo and around the town. For all my keenness to get out of Northern Ireland I found once again that I was actually missing the place. I suppose it was a combination of missing Elizabeth and missing that sense of excitement and focus that fear and tension bring. On top of all that, though, was the question of what I was going to do when my term of service ended in a few months' time. I didn't have a clue. The army hadn't equipped me for anything other than being a soldier. And there was nothing from my old life that I could return to – apart from crime.

I'm not sure who first suggested it as an idea, but in one of my telephone conversations with Elizabeth we started discussing the possibility of my joining the Ulster Defence Regiment. At first I thought it was a mad idea. Apart from Elizabeth there were not too many UDR people I liked and I knew my Irish-Catholic background was a source of discomfort to some of the bigots. But I had heard that quite a few English-born soldiers joined the UDR after serving in Northern Ireland and I began to wonder seriously whether I could make a go of it. Over the following weeks I churned over the idea and, to my surprise, it became more appealing as time went on. I didn't see myself as someone who would make a career of it, but as the horizon seemed empty of other possibilities I thought I could at least do it for a short while. It would offer me a temporary haven while I worked out what I wanted to do with the rest of my life. At least I would be with Elizabeth, in a place I knew, earning money doing the only job I was trained for. It seemed better than being on the dole in Codsall, renewing my acquaintance with the local police. After several weeks of indecision I decided to go for it. I was going to join the UDR.

I had another period of leave due before I left. I wanted to buy a car and drive it over to England. Another soldier, a horrible little Welsh bastard, heard I was looking for one and offered to sell me his. It was a very nice car, albeit left-hand drive, and worth about £3,000. I decided I'd buy it, but as I didn't have that sort of money I asked for a loan from the German bank into which my wages were paid. At first they would not give me it, because they saw I was due to leave the army. But I lied, saying I had just signed up for another three years. Surprisingly they gave me the money without checking my story. I showed the Welshman the loan agreement, but said the money was not going to come through for several weeks. I asked him if in the meantime he would let me take the car with me on leave. He agreed. I didn't tell him the money had already been paid into my account.

Paul was coming with me, and on the ferry over we got extremely drunk. When the boat docked I was asleep in the bar and Paul had collapsed in the shower cubicle in our cabin. It took quite a while for the appeals they were making over the tannoy to penetrate my drunken brain. When I finally realised the registration number they were calling out was my own I ran to the cabin to get Paul. He was totally out of it, so I switched on the shower to wake him up. When the two of us got down to the car deck the place was empty apart from my car. An irritated-looking deck hand came up to us and asked if it was ours. I said it was. He said: "Have you been drinking?" I said: "No, I'm just feeling tired."

I drove off at Harwich at about two o'clock in the morning. I thought I was still in Germany and started driving down the wrong side of the road. It was an easy mistake to make at the time because there were no other cars on the road and my car was left-hand drive. However, I took a bend and saw a car coming towards me on what I thought was the wrong side of the road. I swerved the car between two bollards that were meant to prevent cars driving into a pub car park. Somehow I got through and came to a halt. I jumped out of the car and started shouting at the driver of the other car, which had stopped nearby. I soon realised that he was a policeman. He couldn't work out how I had managed to get through the bollards. He breathalysed me, but amazingly I passed.

"Look, I'm not daft," he said, "I know you've been drinking, even if it hasn't registered." He told me I was not to drive the car again that night. So we slept in the car until the sun came up.

The rest of my leave was spent in a drunken haze: I decided I was going to blow the £3,000 whatever the consequences. I thought that the way I had passed the breathalyser test despite being drunk meant there was something in my metabolism that could allow me to drink as much as I liked and still drive without fear of being done by the police.

On one of the last days of my leave I got in the car after a drinking session. Two friends from home were with me. The windscreen was covered with ice, so I cleared a little slit in the ice to enable me to see. Then I drove off at high speed into the fog. A little way down the road I smashed into the back of a parked car. Unfortunately, there were two people inside, a man and his girlfriend. His head hit the windscreen and was split open, but he wasn't badly hurt. His girlfriend was all right and so was everyone in my car. The police arrived with the breathalyser. I thought I'd pass it easily as I hadn't drunk half as much as before. However, I failed. I was arrested and ended up being fined £250 and banned from driving for 12 months. The car was a write-off and I had spent almost all the £3,000.

Back in Germany I told the car's owner that I'd had a smash in it and that the bank were not releasing the money. I said that when the insurance money came through I would pay him. He wasn't happy, but there was not a lot he could do. I only had a few weeks to do in the army. In the end neither he nor the bank got their money.

In those last few weeks I was called in for a careers-advice chat with a senior officer. I told him I was thinking of joining the UDR. He asked me what else I could do. I said the army had not really equipped me for anything, despite everything they had promised when I had signed up. He suggested I took the test for the higher-grade Class 2 Heavy Goods Vehicle licence (I already held the Class 3). I didn't tell him I was banned from driving. He must have had a word with the army examiner, because my test was very straightforward.

"See if you can drive that," the examiner said, pointing to an amphibious lorry called a Stalwart. I got in and drove it round a field a few times. I didn't take it onto the public highway. After a short while he told me to pull over. I asked him if I had passed the test. "What do you think?" he said.

Before I left I received my Certificate of Service. The range of Military Conduct Gradings is: 1) Exemplary, 2) Very Good, 3) Good, 4) Fair, 5) Unsatisfactory. I was given an "exemplary" grading. The commanding officer added a testimonial:

> O'Mahoney has been in the army since 1979 during which time he has been employed as driver and is qualified to HGV level.

He is a cheerful soldier who can be relied upon to do his best. I have no doubt that he will do well in civilian life as a driver and I would recommend him to any future employer.

With only a short time to go before I left I had let my hair grow longer than the regulation length. I did this deliberately because I didn't want to go back to Northern Ireland with a soldier's short hair-cut. However, a good friend of Nasty's in the regimental police approached me one day and told me to get my hair cut. He was from Northern Ireland himself. I told him why I didn't want to, but he insisted. We had a big argument which resulted in my being arrested for insubordination. I was taken before the troop leader. I explained my reasons for not wanting to cut my hair, but he wouldn't listen. He fined me and ordered me to have my hair cut. I was sure that Nasty had had something to do with it. He knew I was going back to the North and he was probably hoping that republicans would realise I was a squaddie and shoot me. The idea of Fenians shooting a Fenian would have had great appeal to him, especially if he had known what I only discovered myself years later: that "Fenian" – the favourite loyalist nickname for Catholics – came from the activities of one of my nineteenth-century namesakes. John O'Mahoney co-founded and named the IRA's historical forerunner, the Fenian Brotherhood (later notorious for the so-called "Fenian Rising" of 1867). I don't think Johnno was from our branch of the family, but I might have met him once at a party.

The night before I left Germany my troop held a farewell party for me at which I got quite drunk. The party came to a raucous end when Paul and others announced that they had a surprise for me. The room full of soldiers and wives fell silent as Paul said that they had flown over a special lady to be with me for the evening. Everyone thought he was about to introduce Elizabeth. The the door flew open and a full-size blow-up doll was thrown into the room. It was wearing a mini-skirt and a T-shirt bearing on its front the logo of the *Liverpool Echo* newspaper and on the back the words "I get it six nights a week." For some reason this seemed to upset some of the wives and the party ended. Paul and I were staggering back to our room without our inflatable friend when Nasty came towards us. I still had the hump with him over the hair-cutting incident. "You off tomorrow then, Fenian? he said.

"Fuck off," I said.

"What did you say?"

"I said fuck off. Have you got a problem with that?"

He just stood there as I walked towards him. When I got about six feet away he backed off, saying: "Don't start, O'Mahoney. Or you'll be locked up tomorrow instead of going home." I knew his bottle had gone, just as it had gone when we had come under fire in Northern Ireland. Paul wanted to bash him as well but we knew he would have grassed us up, so we left it.

Then the next day I flew back to Northern Ireland.

18

Your P45 Is with the ASU

IARRIVED in Fermanagh for Christmas. It was good to see Elizabeth again, but I felt strange walking around as an ordinary civilian. I moved into Elizabeth's flat in the centre of Enniskillen, near the Watergate Bridge just opposite the castle. Until that time her mother, father and brother had been an invisible presence, appearing occasionally in conversation, but never in the flesh. That was about to change: I had been invited to spend Christmas Day with them. I knew her father was a retired RUC officer and that her brother had followed him into the police. I also knew her mother was a devoted follower of the Reverend Ian Paisley. I remembered how she had stood unsuccessfully as a Democratic Unionist Party candidate in the May council elections. Beyond those bare facts I knew little else.

I got an inkling of troubled times ahead when Elizabeth sat me down and told me she wanted to explain a few things before I met her family. She said her mother had quite extreme views on a number of issues and, however ridiculous I found them, she would like me to respect them. In essence her mother was a fundamentalist Protestant who didn't like having anything to do with Catholics. Nor did she want her children having any such dealings. Elizabeth said she could not be honest with her mother about my background: in her mother's eyes, because I'd been born a Catholic, I would always be a Catholic, at least until I had been re-baptised as a born-again Protestant. I had never really liked the term "born a Catholic". I was not born a Catholic. I was born naked and screaming. My religion had been imposed upon me. If I'd been born in India I would have been a Sikh or a Hindu or a Moslem. The only God I had ever worshipped was George Best – and he was an Ulster Protestant.

Elizabeth knew my views and agreed with them to a large extent, but she asked me, for the sake of family harmony, to keep my Catholic background secret. In fact she wanted me to lie. She knew her mother would pick up on my Catholic name, so she suggested a cover story. If asked, I was to say that my family came originally from southern Ireland but had been Protestants for generations, the stain of Catholicism having been expunged long ago. Her other stricture was that I had to make sure I didn't swear or blaspheme in front of her mother. I said: "Of course I'm not going to swear!" But she explained that, for her mother, swearing and blaspheming came together in the use of such words as "Jesus", "God" or "bloody". Nor could I expect to drink alcohol in her mother's house – or even give the impression that I had ever drunk alcohol anywhere in the world at any time. Apart from all that, she thought I'd get on fine.

Elizabeth's parents' bungalow stood in a valley beside a lake with breath-taking views all round. I felt deeply uncomfortable as I walked up the pathway to the front door clutching a bottle of non-alcoholic drink. It was not the natural discomfort everyone feels before a first meeting with a partner's parents. It was more the uncomfortable feeling of knowing that, quite literally, I could not be myself. I told myself it was only for a day: I might not have to meet them ever again.

The mother greeted us at the door. She was friendly, but reserved. I recognised her from her photo on the election leaflet. She was very softly spoken and the personification of good manners. She was slim, about 5ft 8in, with silver-white hair. She brought us into the sitting room. I wish Elizabeth had prepared me for it. I was faced with what I can only describe as a shrine to Ian Paisley. His face beamed out from numerous photos in which he was often standing alongside Elizabeth's mother. There was even a photo of the two of them together in that very room. Photos of the Queen and the royal family were also prominent, along with lots of little figurines and knick-knacks of historical figures such as King William of Orange.

Elizabeth's dad was sitting in one of the armchairs. He was about 60, short, thick set with large gnarled hands. His white hair was balding. He got up to shake my hand and I noticed he had a bad limp. I found out later that this resulted from a wound received when the IRA blew up his Land Rover with a culvert bomb. Over dinner his wife said he had been taken to a hospital where, she claimed, he had been refused treatment by the Fenians who worked there. He had been airlifted to Belfast and had ended up being pensioned off. He was extremely quiet and hardly ever spoke. I think he was shy. When I met him in the future he would sometimes go into the garden to speak to Elizabeth or his wife.

Over dinner the conversation was polite and stilted. I was extremely edgy, worried I would say something to identify me as a Fenian interloper. I sipped my ginger beer temperately, trying to anticipate the mother's questions so I could give myself time to prepare acceptable answers. She asked me what an Englishman was doing in Fermanagh. I realised Elizabeth had told her almost nothing about me. I described my army background and the recent tour of duty. I said I had enjoyed being in Northern Ireland and had decided to return in order to join Elizabeth in the UDR. The atmosphere changed almost immediately. I found her warming to me and, strangely, I found myself warming to her. She was lively and intelligent and not without humour: she could speak knowledgeably on many subjects. She talked a bit about her involvement in local politics, although I think she tended to assume a background knowledge I didn't have. She told me how in the sixties she had wrapped herself in the Union Flag and lain in the road to block a Civil Rights march by Catholics. She had been shocked when police moved her out the way. I was probably being overly sensitive, but I had the feeling she was analysing every word we said for signs of Catholicism or blasphemy. For instance, I might have said: "My friend Patrick has got one of those cars." And she would have said: "Patrick? That's a Catholic name. Is Patrick a Catholic?"

After dinner we sat down again in the sitting room to watch the Queen's Speech. It was a first for me. Fortunately, they kept the television on after the speech, so at least I had a little respite from talking and the constant danger of betraying myself. But there were dangers in watching television too. Something happened on screen which made me say: "Oh, God! I don't believe it." Elizabeth's mother breathed in sharply, clutched her chest and walked out. Elizabeth whispered angrily: "I told you not to swear."

I tried to settle down into my new life with Elizabeth, but there was an uneasiness in our relationship which had not been apparent before. Perhaps it was my fault. I had expected something different from my new life. I suppose I had almost expected to have my old army life back, but with more perks, such as the freedom to live outside camp with a woman I was fond of. But life as a civilian was very different. None of my friends were around and even from those very first days I began to feel extremely isolated. This sense of isolation would only intensify over time. In truth, the appeal of this new start began to evaporate rapidly. I tried to enjoy myself, but deep down I knew I had made a mistake in going back.

Shortly after my arrival I went to the main RUC station in Enniskillen and enquired about obtaining a firearms licence. If the Provos did pay me a visit I wanted at least to have the chance to defend myself. The policeman at the desk summoned a colleague who dealt with such applications. He asked me why I wanted one. I explained my background and what I was doing in Northern Ireland. He nodded sympathetically and said he didn't think that, as a former soldier, I would have any problems. He asked me various questions from a prepared list: was I on any medication? Had

235

I ever received treatment for, or been diagnosed as having, a mental illness? I got through everything all right until he came to the question I had been dreading: had I ever been convicted of a criminal offence? I suppose I could have lied, but I knew that, as a matter of course, he would run my name through the police computer and find my record. Then I would have committed another criminal offence by lying to obtain a firearm. So I told the truth. I said I'd faced a few minor charges. He asked what they were. I said: "Eh, assault, robbery, theft, threatening behaviour, possessing an offensive weapon and criminal damage." His manner became a little frosty. He told me I would be wasting my time applying: there was no way that someone with my record would be given a firearms licence. I was annoyed. I said I had only recently spent four and a half months patrolling Fermanagh with a firearm. He shrugged his shoulders.

I had better luck with the UDR. Elizabeth brought home an application form for me which I completed immediately. I was worried the UDR would use the RUC's computer to check me out. Around three weeks later I received a letter asking me to come for interview. I returned to St Angelo and was interviewed by a UDR captain. He was relaxed and informal. He talked to me about my recent tour of duty and asked after one of my regiment's officers. He asked me why I wanted to join the UDR. I said I had thoroughly enjoyed my time in Northern Ireland and wanted to make a go of living there. He seemed happy enough with my replies and said that my application would be sent away for processing, but that he saw no obvious problems. The processing took a few months. Elizabeth came home one day and told me the outcome: I had been accepted into the UDR. I rang the captain who said I would be joining the new intake in September/October. He apologised for the fact that I'd have to wait so long, but he said the delay was unavoidable.

I liked Elizabeth immensely. She was a lovely person, kind and gentle, and a lot of the time we got on fine, but we came from such different backgrounds that inevitably I began to feel how alien we were to each other. In the past at St Angelo she had laughed with me at the stupidity of some of the sectarian bigots at the base. She had often said: "We're not all like that." But living with her and meeting her friends and family I felt at times the evidence told me different. She certainly didn't hate Catholics, but the world she lived in had been formed by the Troubles. Almost all her friends and family were involved with the security forces in one way or another. They saw themselves as frontierspeople barricading their homesteads against marauding natives. It was all hands to the pump-action shotgun. Religion, or rather the religious denomination of others, dominated Elizabeth's thoughts and those of all her friends. Yet few of them seemed to practise their religion; few went to church or bible meetings or anything like that. The words "Protestant" and "Catholic" were used simply to identify friends from enemies, people whose company you could embrace from those whose company you had to shun.

Elizabeth was far more liberal than the others for whom "Catholic" – any sort of Catholic – meant "republican", meant "the enemy". She could distinguish between Irish Catholics (or at least Irish-born Catholics, republicans, the enemy) and English Catholics and even English-born Irish Catholics like me. However, I felt that a lot of her friends, especially those from St Angelo who knew about my background, did not accept me. My blood tainted me; and even my prospective

UDR uniform could not redeem me. We used to go to a particular pub in the area that was popular with UDR and RUC people. I had a few good evenings there, but the pattern was always the same. I would meet new people one evening, and we'd get on great, but the next time we met they'd be cold and distant, as if they had been warned off me. Elizabeth would sometimes say I was imagining things, but I knew I wasn't. The fact was that I could see from Elizabeth's own behaviour how whispers about someone's untrustworthiness could start. Sometimes we used to go round to the house of one of her friends. This friend used to share the house with her sister who, so far as I could see, seemed to spend her days sewing. Before we went there for the first time Elizabeth told me I was not to say anything to the sister. I asked her why. She said: "She's not to be trusted. She mixes with the wrong people." When I asked her to explain further all she could say was that this woman occasionally drank in Catholic pubs and had Catholic friends.

I could understand the need for constant vigilance; I knew that careless cops and squaddies ended up dead, but at the same time I felt she was security-conscious to the point of obsession. Worse – she expected me to be the same. It began to put a strain on our relationship. She would always be appealing to me to think of the minutiae of personal security. I soon felt I was being nagged. She started to drive me mad with her list of things I could and couldn't do – you can't go here, you can't go there, you can't do this, you can't do that. I had never liked being told what to do – and there was nothing more likely to make me do the opposite. She kept telling me about one particular pub near the flat that I had to avoid. From the way she described it you would have thought it was the headquarters of the IRA's Northern Command. She warned me so often not to go in there that I developed a real urge to see what it was like. One day I just thought: "Fuck it. I'm going in." Inside were six old men supping Guinness and listening to diddly-diddly music. I ended up getting half-drunk with them. They were very friendly. They asked me what I was doing over there. I said I'd come over for the fishing, which a lot of English people did. Elizabeth was annoyed when I told her. She kept saying: "You shouldn't have done that. You'll end up dead if they find out what you are."

I don't want to give the impression I was fearless – I wasn't by any means. In fact I regarded myself as extremely security-conscious. For instance, to get to the flat you had to go through a wooden door off the street into a courtyard then up some stairs to the rooms. In the living room was a set of large glass double-doors which opened onto a garden which backed into an alleyway where the public had right of way. I insisted the curtains were kept closed at all times, because I thought if gunmen attacked they would come up the alley into the garden and through those doors. Sitting watching TV with the light on and the curtains open would have meant the gunmen would not even have had to bother entering the flat. I also tied cotton around the back gate and checked it a couple of times a week to see if it had been broken by anyone coming in to snoop around. I would also walk past the flat entrance on the street if somebody was walking behind me. I would walk up the road, cross, look in a shop window for a while and walk back down. I didn't do all this because Elizabeth told me to. I did it because I had been brainwashed by the army into seeing death and danger everywhere and in everyone. It made me angry, and sometimes I felt stupid, but I knew it was necessary. So to have Elizabeth then tell me I wasn't doing enough to protect myself irritated me. Vigilance was essential, but not to the point where your quality of life disappeared.

Elizabeth was very close to her family and we started to see quite a lot of her parents and brother. The latter was in the RUC, based in Enniskillen. He was about 35, tall and slim with a moustache. His wife was a nice woman, very approachable and thoughtful. She was very close to Elizabeth, who even told her the truth about my background. The wife assured me once that she would never disclose my secret, not even to her husband. I was surprised at this, because he struck me as one of the nicest policemen I had ever met. He didn't seem to harbour any dark thoughts about anyone. Sometimes we would visit them at their modest three-bedroomed house on the outskirts of Enniskillen. Elizabeth felt at ease there with her brother's wife, but I sensed the latter somehow felt guilty that I was there talking to her husband who didn't know "the truth" about me. I doubt whether he would have cared, but he might himself then have felt guilty about keeping "the truth" from his mother. I often felt as if I had done something awful. I sometimes bumped into Elizabeth's brother as he patrolled the town centre. I saw at first hand the decent way he treated and spoke to people, Catholic and Protestant.

One peculiar development was that I started getting on really well with the mother. I suppose she had never met anyone like me before and I used to make her laugh. She would greet me with real warmth and affection. She genuinely liked me and I genuinely liked her, which began to sadden me. I felt like a lying Judas. Yet I knew that if I told her I had been born a Catholic her attitude towards me would have done an about-turn. She would have treated me like a nasty disease, despite the fact that in flesh, blood, mind and spirit I would have been no different from the person she had grown fond of. I have heard black people talk about white racism, but to me this was more poisonous – and less understandable. It was a seething hatred for others born on the same small island, in the same town, even in the same hospital or street, and sharing the same language, accent and skin colour. Sometimes I used to tell Elizabeth I was going to reveal to her mother the truth about myself. She wouldn't believe me. Then I would sit in the lounge with the two of them and, looking first at Elizabeth, I would say to her mother: "I've never told you this before, but I'm. . ." The colour would drain from Elizabeth's face as she looked at me in disbelief. Then I'd say something like, ". . . I'm a . . . thinking of taking time out to go to America." Elizabeth's face would almost sag with relief. I would roar with laughter, whatever response her mother gave.

I felt like a phoney hiding behind an assumed identity. I couldn't tell anyone, Protestant or Catholic, who I really was. It began to get me down, which was dangerous, because when I feel that way I tend to turn those feelings into anger which I direct outwards at the world. One evening when Elizabeth wasn't at home I felt particularly down. I began feeling angry at being surrounded by all this phoniness. As a joke someone had given me a little blue-and-white shield-shaped badge on which was emblazoned the provocative symbol of militant loyalism, the Red Hand of Ulster. I stuck it on my jacket and went for a drink in another Provo pub that Elizabeth had warned me to steer clear of. The pub was only about a quarter full. I stood at the bar waiting to be served, my badge of defiance unnoticed by the elderly regulars. I couldn't see what Elizabeth was fussing about:

none of the customers in this supposed IRA den looked violent or capable of violence.

The barman, a stocky Lenin lookalike, came and said politely: "And what can I get for you, sir?" His eyes fell on my badge. It was like a crucifix to the Anti-Christ. I saw his eyes widening then he shouted at me: "Get out of here with that thing on."

I told him I wasn't going anywhere: I wanted a drink. He continued shouting at me to get out, but I refused. The customers watched me with silent hostility, but no-one intervened. The barman said he was calling the police, an unusual act for a republican, but I assumed that the hated symbol of loyalism on my jacket had unhinged him. Within a short while two armed policemen came into the pub. I explained the situation, but they told me a landlord was under no obligation to serve anyone. They asked me to leave with them.

Outside one of them said: "You shouldn't go in there, especially not wearing that badge."

I said: "If I want to wear a badge I'll wear a fucking badge and they won't stop me." He said again that I shouldn't return to that pub. I said I was sick of being told where I could and couldn't go: "I'll go where I want." I didn't tell Elizabeth what I'd done, but within a few days she knew. Word had got back to her, even though I hadn't known those policemen. She could not believe I had been so stupid.

Elizabeth realised I wasn't happy. I could tell she was worried about the way I was drawing attention to myself. She would try to remind me that I wasn't in England where my loutish behaviour might only provoke a fist-fight: "Over here they'll learn who you are, what you are, wait for their moment and shoot you. You've got to take it easy. You've got to learn your boundaries." That weekend she suggested we got out of Enniskillen for the day. We went across the border to a nearby town to see a concert by an Irish country band led by someone called Big Tom. It was not my sort of music, but Elizabeth was keen. Inside the venue, peculiarly, the audience sat down to a meal of fish and chips before the band came on. While I was eating, a man walked past and jogged the table, spilling my pint of beer. He didn't apologise. I thought it was a deliberate act to provoke me. By now I believed it was me versus the whole of Ulster.

"Oi, you prick," I shouted after him, "you spilt my beer."

He didn't even look around. Elizabeth told me to forget about it, but I was furious. I got up and approached the man who had moved to stand a few yards away. I told him he had spilt my beer and that I wanted another pint. He stared at me without saying anything. "Look, tosser," I said, "are you going to buy me another pint?" Again he didn't say anything and just stared at me vacantly. I grabbed him by the lapels of his jacket and pulled him close to my face. I shouted: "Answer me! Answer me!"

A woman came rushing over to me: "Leave him alone! Leave him alone! He's deaf and dumb."

I sat back down next to Elizabeth, who looked horror-struck at the attention I had drawn to us. Fortunately the band started playing.

Elizabeth must have thought I needed to be kept away from large groups of people, because she suggested we moved out of Enniskillen into the countryside. An ex-UDR man owned a house in a remote area near Maguiresbridge and he said he'd rent it to us. I fancied a change, but when I saw the house I

243

wasn't sure it was quite the change I needed. We were about half a mile from the nearest neighbours, a mile from the main road and five miles from the nearest village. Worst of all, we were practically on the border, making us easy targets for the IRA. However, Elizabeth seemed to think it was a good idea, so I went along with her.

I had been back in Northern Ireland for about three months by this stage. There were still several months to go before I joined the UDR. I had not bothered looking for work, because I didn't want to be in a position where an employer would have to receive my P45 (the official certificate detailing my last employment). But boredom was really beginning to bite and I decided to see if the dole office offered any back-to-work re-training courses at the local college. I went to a dole office that Elizabeth had told me was "safe" (that is, the one most likely to have Protestant staff and a Protestant clientele). They found me a place on an engineering course at a college in Enniskillen. Memories of my schooldays filled me with dread, but I thought the course would at least get me out of the house. I had arranged that my P45 from the army would be sent to the Department of Employment, which would effectively be my employer during my time on the course.

I discovered that most of my fellow students were Catholics, as was the instructor. On the first day he went around the class asking people about themselves. Perhaps I was paranoid, but he seemed to pay special attention to me. I suppose I was an oddity, because there were not too many people with English accents in the college. He asked me what I was doing over there. I said my parents were Irish; they had moved back to Ireland and I had decided to join them. I hoped that would be enough for him, but he kept asking searching questions. Where were my parents from? What did my dad do? Where were they living? Perhaps he was just being pally, but he made me feel uncomfortable. The other students weren't particularly friendly, although that could have been my fault as I was not overly friendly myself. I wasn't looking for a new group of mates. I felt that, even though they knew I had Irish blood, for them the most important fact about me was my English accent.

Later in the week as we sat in the classroom before the start of the lesson the instructor said clearly in front of the class: "Bernard, could you come to the office later? Your P45 has arrived from the army."

I thought: "I'm fucked." I felt like punching the bastard in the face, but I just gave a little laugh and said: "No problem." I knew he had done it on purpose. At the time I thought he was trying to cause me problems – and I even considered giving him a bashing – but with hindsight I think he might have been trying to do me a favour by letting me know that other people, apart from himself, could already have seen the P45. From then on the instructor remained friendly – more proof that I had more to fear from "nice" people – but almost all the other students made a point of ignoring me. The only people who would ever speak to me were Protestants, and there weren't many of them around. Within days someone had scrawled "Brits Out" on the back of my overalls. I would come in to find my bits of practical work smashed to pieces or missing. I felt vulnerable, but angry. I used to make sure I carried a sharp tool around with me at all times. I was waiting for someone to say or do something overtly hostile – so I could justifiably smash his face in.

One day as I was standing at the college gates I noticed a motorbike driving past. The pillion passenger stared at me.

The bike went up the road and drove into a garage forecourt. It turned around and came back down past me. Again the pillion passenger stared at me. The bike stopped at the end of the road. I thought they were just two students who were going to have a go at me. I felt my temper rising. I started walking towards them, thinking, "If they want it, they can have it." They must have seen the look on my face, because as I came within 20 yards they drove off. I told Elizabeth about it: she immediately assumed they were Provos carrying out surveillance on me. She told her brother, who assumed the same. He wanted me to leave the college immediately. I didn't want to: I wasn't going to run from them. He said: "Well, you've really got to start being careful." I did become a lot more careful. I didn't think they would risk doing anything to me inside the complex, but outside was different. I tried to alternate between different exits and I would walk away in different directions. Elizabeth used to pick me up at pre-arranged places.

To make matters worse, around this time strange things started happening at the new house. Our dog, Jagger, started barking occasionally during the night, as if there was someone outside. Then one night when we were in bed I heard the sound of a car driving up to the house. Someone got out and banged on the front door. Elizabeth had always told me never to open the door after 10 p.m. She and her friends had an agreement that they would never call on each other after that time, except in emergencies – and only then if they had telephoned first. We stayed where we were, knowing it could only be a stranger. Elizabeth didn't have a personal firearm. She knew there was no point in applying for one if she was sharing a house with someone with my criminal record. There were a few more bangs and Jagger was barking madly. Then we heard a car door slamming and the car driving away. I said to Elizabeth that the driver was probably lost and looking for directions. But I knew I was really just telling myself what I wanted to hear. These were only small things, but they began to play on both our minds. A few weeks later we came home to find that someone had painted the word "scum" in large capital letters on the front door. Elizabeth – if this was possible – became even more security-conscious. So did I. I seemed to spend my days asking myself questions like: "Who's that looking at me? Should I check under the car again? Did I leave the gate closed like that? Did I take this route last time?" But at times I would feel sick of living like that and I would drop my guard and maybe do something that Elizabeth regarded as incautious. All of this put a tremendous strain on us and the relationship began deteriorating rapidly. Ironically, her mother, who didn't even know we were living together – she thought I was still based at St Angelo – started dropping hints about our getting married. She would say things like: "Oh, you and Elizabeth are getting on well. I'll introduce you to the minister." or "I hope you're not going to wear boots to the wedding. Ha! Ha! Ha!" I thought: "Wedding? What wedding?"

But everything came to a sudden end. I came out of college one day to find two green RUC Cortinas with bullet-proof windows parked outside. Elizabeth was standing in the road between them talking to two policemen. A UDR friend was with her. She was crying. I thought something drastic had happened. I ran to her and said: "What's wrong? What's wrong?" "You've got to go," she said. "You've just got to go."

I asked her what she meant. One of the policemen said it was best that we didn't go back to the house. I asked him why.

He said that things had been happening and they were advising me to go. "Go where?" I asked.

He said it had been arranged that I would go back to England for a few weeks: Elizabeth would join me later and everything would be fine.

"I'm not going anywhere," I said.

But he was firmly insistent: "It's for your own good. We're going to drive you to the ferry now."

I could hardly believe what was happening. I said: "What about my gear?" He said they had put all my gear in the boot. I just caved in: I felt I had no choice in the matter. The fact was that I did have no choice in the matter. Elizabeth was still crying. I kissed her goodbye. She said she would come over to England to see me soon. I got in one of the police cars and we drove off. They drove me to Larne to get the ferry to Stranraer in Scotland. I only discovered then that they had not brought all my possessions. They had filled three cases, but most of the stuff I'd brought from England had been left behind: around 300 LPs, several hundred singles, all my photos and books, my army reserve kit, a lot of my clothes and other personal bits and pieces. There was nothing I could do about it now. I was too dazed to complain. I just got on the ferry. It set sail. For the whole journey I stood on the deck watching the shores of Northern Ireland slowly disappear.

I never received a satisfactory explanation for why the RUC became involved in taking me to Larne. The more I thought about it, the more extraordinary it seemed. If they had thought we were in immediate danger they could just have helped us move that day to somewhere else in Enniskillen. Why did I need to be moved out of the country while Elizabeth stayed behind? And surely – no matter how immediate the danger –

they could have consulted the two of us to enable us to decide what we wanted to do? Elizabeth did come over to England a few times. I tried to get to the bottom of what had happened, but she would say either that she didn't know or that she didn't want to talk about it. The first and most detailed explanation she gave me was that she had kept her brother informed of everything that was going on – the men on the motorbike, the bang on the door, the graffiti on the house – and he had told his superiors, who thought I needed to be moved back to England immediately for my own safety. At first I chose to believe that explanation, but over time it became more implausible.

I came to feel that what had probably happened was that her parents had found out about my Catholic background and the fact that we were living in sin – and they had wanted me out of her life. The apparent danger I was putting her in with my occasional foolish behaviour would merely have added to their determination to remove me physically from Fermanagh. I was sure the family's RUC connections would easily have provided the clout to arrange for me to be taken to Larne and put on a boat. I couldn't help feeling that Elizabeth had played a part in what had happened. At the very least she had been complicit. The relationship, based as it was on a multitude of falsehoods, had become greatly strained. It wouldn't have lasted, but at the same time I hadn't wanted it to end the way it did.

Elizabeth told me that my possessions had been put at her parents' house for safe-keeping. I was planning to pick them up myself eventually. When I saw Elizabeth in England about six months later I mentioned I would have to get my stuff back from her parents' house urgently: I was missing my records and

I needed my clothing and personal effects. I had mentioned the subject several times before and she had behaved oddly, as if she were trying to change the subject. This time, however, she could tell I wanted to make firm arrangements for the return of what was mine. She looked a bit embarrassed. Then she said her parents had destroyed everything. I was stunned. I asked her why. She said they didn't think I was coming back. I wanted to know why she or they hadn't contacted me before doing something so drastic. Again she couldn't, or wouldn't, give me a satisfactory explanation.

I felt angry and upset. I had lost almost all my most personal possessions. Not just records and clothes, but photos and letters – things that were irreplaceable. It confirmed to me that her family had discovered that I'd been lying to them about my background. I imagined how shocked her poor mother must have been to discover she had been trying to marry her daughter off to a Fenian. I thought of her falling to her knees and praying to God or the Reverend Ian Paisley, or both, in abject apology for her wickedness. I could imagine her, too, piling up my possessions in her garden, dousing them with petrol and, in an act of cathartic cleansing, flicking a lighted match onto the heap.

In the future my journey would take me to some strange and violent places where I would mix with some strange and violent people, yet nothing would compare with the dangerous peculiarity of that truncated corner of Ulster. With my Irish blood and my British upbringing I should have felt at home there. But I had never felt, and would never feel, so alien. As I imagined my possessions going up in flames my anger was tempered by a sense of relief. I would never return there. They were welcome to their bonfires.

SOME OTHER READING
from
BRANDON

EAMONN MCCANN

Bloody Sunday in Derry
What Really Happened

On 30th January 1972 the Parachute Regiment shot twenty-seven unarmed civil rights demonstrators in Derry. Fourteen men and boys died on what has come to be known as Bloody Sunday.

At the heart of the book are fourteen pieces about those who died. Each is an account by a relative, friend, neighbour or other associate of the dead person. There is also a compelling account of the events of that day and their aftermath, and a detailed analysis of the Widgery Report, which, it concludes, was the single greatest travesty of justice arising out of the Northern Ireland turmoil of the past three decades.

"This moving and impressive book is cumulatively powerful. The *tour de force* of the book is its description of Lord Widgery's Tribunal. As a mendacious and arrogant piece of judicial trumpery, it can hardly be equalled." *Guardian*

"Nobody should moralise about the Northern Troubles without reading it." *Phoenix*

"A highly successful formula of 'unsanitised' primary sources, oral history and political commentary and analysis. The layout of the book makes for easy reading of a complex and disturbing truth." *Books Ireland*

ISBN 0 86322 274 9; Paperback £9.99

GERRY ADAMS

An Irish Voice
The Quest for Peace

with an introduction by Niall O'Dowd

"The importance of this collection from one of the foremost revolutionary figures of the late 20th century becomes immediately evident . . . And, as these articles show, he is a thinker of considerable stature . . . *An Irish Voice* is a good read. For the humour as much as the philosophy or the politics." Tim Pat Coogan, *The Irish Times*

ISBN 1 902011 01 5; Paperback £9.99

STEVE MACDONOGH
Open Book: One Publisher's War

"MacDonogh is without doubt the most adventurous and determined of the Irish publishers . . . This is an important book." *Phoenix*

"A fascinating and very important book." Brid Rosney, Today FM

"The parallels between Orwell and MacDonogh are striking . . . MacDonogh's transparent writing is redolent of Orwell's famous 'plain style'. Most significant of all, . . . Orwell believed that the fate of democracy is linked with that of literature. MacDonogh's career is an illustration of that point . . . *Open Book* is an intelligent, informative account of a life spent fighting for freedom of speech, a right which is still not adequately safeguarded." *Irish World*

"Fascinating reading." *Sunday Business Post*

ISBN 0 86322 263 3; Paperback £8.99

ALISON O'CONNOR

A Message from Heaven
The Life and Crimes of Father Sean Fortune

A prize-winning young journalist tells the extraordinary story of a master manipulator

In the long list of Irish paedophile priests Fr Sean Fortune occupies a pre-eminent position. Sexual abuse of children was his worst crime, but far from his only one. Fortune, a master manipulator, capable of incredible charm, left a trail of destruction in his wake. He lied, cheated, bullied and abused. He loved the limelight. His cunning kept him one step ahead of the pack. Some of his activities were so bizarre as to make them incredible.

When Fortune committed suicide in March 1999, he left behind a poem which he had titled: "A Message from Heaven to My Family". He also left behind many victims. Not least among these were eight young men who had come forward and made statements to the police about their sexual abuse. His death meant that they will now forever remain the "alleged victims" of Father Sean Fortune.

Alison O'Connor is a journalist with *The Irish Times*. For her coverage of Fr Fortune's life and times she was awarded a 1999 ESB National Media Award.

ISBN 0 86322 270 6; Paperback £9.99

SEAN O'CALLAGHAN

To Hell or Barbados
The ethnic cleansing of Ireland

Between 1652 and 1659 over 50,000 Irish men, women and children were transported to Barbados and Virginia. Yet until now there has been no account of what became of them.

The motivation for the initial transportation of the Irish was expressed by King James I of England: "Root out the Papists and fill it [Ireland] with Protestants."

The author's search began in the library of the Barbados Museum and Historical Society and its files on Irish slaves. Sean O'Callaghan for the first time documents the history of these people: their transportation, the conditions in which they lived on plantations as slaves or servants, and their rebellions in Barbados.

Sean O'Callaghan is the author of fourteen previous books, including *The Slave Trade in Africa*, which was translated into thirteen languages and filmed by Malenotti of Rome.

ISBN 0 86322 272 2; Hardback £15.99